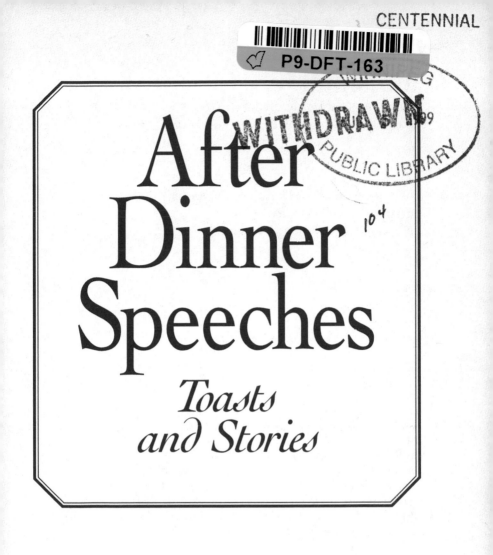

# After Dinner Speeches

## Toasts and Stories

# foulsham
LONDON • NEW YORK • TORONTO • SYDNEY

# foulsham

The Publishing House, Bennetts Close,
Cippenham, Slough, Berkshire, SL1 5AP, England

Some material originally published under the titles
*Successful Speeches & Toasts* and
*Speeches and Toasts for all Occasions.*

ISBN 0-572-02416-9

Printed in Great Britain by St. Edmundsbury Press, Bury St. Edmunds

# Contents

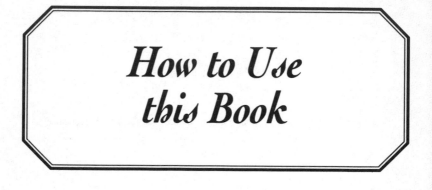

# How to Use this Book

**O**ratory is a gift, but the ability to make a competent speech in public can be readily acquired. This book does not pretend to teach its readers to become brilliant orators. It is a practical and comprehensive guide to speaking, and its sole object is to help the inexperienced to make a good, competent speech on any occasion.

Whatever kind of speech you have to make, first read Chapter 1. Next look through the list of contents to see if a specimen of your speech is included. Even if it is not, you will probably find one that comes close to it, because the specimens have been carefully chosen to cover a wide field.

Having found your speech, or one closely allied to it, first read any hints at the beginning and then read the specimen. Finally, run your eye down the list of useful quotations below the specimen. Then go back to Chapter 1 and carry out the instructions for preparing the speech that you will deliver.

You could, of course, use the specimen exactly as it stands, but this is not recommended – it is better to use it as the basis for a speech which you write yourself. There are several reasons for this. The most important reason is that the speech you make should be phrased in a style similar to that of your ordinary conversation. You may want to make a slightly longer speech than most of the specimens, and you will probably want to include a few personal details, and perhaps a humorous story. The specimens provided follow the traditional and formal format and may seem a little too formal for your usual way of speaking. You should, of course, modify them to suit your own style.

If you have to make a speech on a special subject that is not included among the specimens, read Chapters 1 and 2. Here detailed advice on the preparation of a longer speech is given in such a form that it can be adapted to almost any kind of speech that you are required to make.

Chapter 2 is intended mainly for those who are required to make specialised speeches on subjects not covered in the specimens in this book. If your speech is covered (or if you can find a specimen on a closely related subject) you do not have to study this chapter, although it does contain much information likely to be of general use to every speaker.

After you have prepared your speech along the lines suggested in Chapter 1 and a specimen, or in Chapters 1 and 2, go on to Chapter 3 for instructions on delivery. These apply equally to all speeches and toasts.

If you have been called upon to take the chair at a meeting or function, turn to Chapter 4.

A selection of additional general quotations is given at the end of the book. Both these and the useful quotations given under the various specimens should be used with care. General advice on the use of quotations is included in Chapter 1.

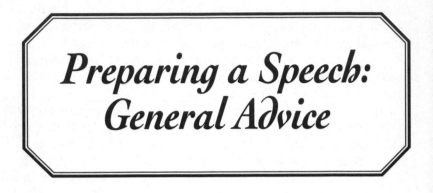

# CHAPTER ONE

# *Preparing a Speech: General Advice*

Speeches are meant to be heard, not read. This may seem obvious, but a good speech cannot be prepared unless this fact is constantly kept in mind.

You may hear a public speech that impresses you very much. Then you may read the same speech in a newspaper and wonder why you were so affected by it. The speech that sounded so brilliant might seem quite mediocre in print. Perhaps you will conclude that it was the manner of the delivery and the personality of the speaker that made it sound so much better than it reads, but this is rarely the complete explanation. The fact is that it was prepared to be heard, not read – that it was designed to catch the ear, not the eye.

If you reverse the process, and try to prepare a speech by writing an article and then saying this aloud to an audience, you will not have much success as a speaker. It may be a very good article, but it will not be a good speech. What is more, you will realise this yourself as you deliver it.

In certain respects, however, good speeches and good articles have points in common. Both should be clear, not muddled; the arrangements of facts and arguments should be orderly and logical; there should be no waste of words or digression; and the style should be simple and direct.

# First Steps

This first chapter is concerned with all speeches and toasts, and the hints will be general. Chapter 2 will give detailed instructions on preparing a speech of some length and importance on a special subject.

The first thing to bear in mind is that whatever the nature of the speech or toast, it needs preparation in advance. Some people can get up and make an extempore speech, but those who do this well are usually those who have had experience of public speaking. If you know in advance that you are going to be called on to make a speech don't leave your preparation until the last minute. Don't imagine that you will be able to 'rise to the occasion' without having given it any thought before, because you probably won't.

First, think of your subject, and decide what it is you want to say. Lodge this firmly into your mind – and then write it down on paper. You will probably have several ideas, so write them all down. Then put them in order so that one follows on from another. Cut out repetition and irrelevance. If your speech includes facts, check up to make sure you have got them right.

Eventually you should be able to boil down your ideas to the form of short notes. From these you can write out a model speech. Keep your notes; guidance on how to use these and the model speech will be given in Chapter 3. The speech will, of course, need revising several times. It is best to write it quickly, and it will help considerably if you say it aloud as you write it down. For, as was said at the beginning of this chapter, a speech is not an article. It is meant to be heard, not read, and the surest guide is that if it sounds right it is right. Never mind what it looks like. Continue to say the words aloud when you revise the speech. You will be surprised to find how different they seem when they are heard instead of seen.

# Yourself and your Audience

In preparing the speech you must consider both yourself and your audience. Remember that you have to deliver the speech. You know your ability to express things, and you know your limitations. Make concessions to them. Do not set yourself a task that is too hard. It is no good composing a beautiful speech if it is so beautiful it becomes impossible for you to deliver it properly.

Consideration of your audience calls for a good deal of thought. Obviously there will be a significant difference in style between a speech made at a regimental dinner and an address at a Women's Institute. That is an exaggerated example, and in any case it is hardly likely that your subject would be the same on both occasions. Naturally the subject determines the style to a certain extent, but you must also consider what sort of people there will be in your audience. Consider their age, their sex, the social status and especially their relationship to you. If you know most of them by their forenames, don't speak to them as if they were all complete strangers. If you don't know any of them, don't try to pretend that you do, even by implication.

Be sincere. Don't say something that you don't believe because it won't ring true, and it is insulting to your audience. Omit anything that might cause offence, but don't say something just to please them unless you can say it with honesty and sincerity.

## Brevity and Simplicity

Be brief. You rarely hear complaints about a speech being too short, but you hear many people complain that a speech was too long. If you are given a time limit, keep to it. If you are not given a time limit, set one for yourself – and keep to it. Remember that when timing yourself you must make liberal allowances for pauses and – it is to be hoped – for applause and laughter. It is better to finish before your time is up than to go beyond the limit.

Always write your speech in short sentences. They are easier to remember, easier to deliver, and easier for your listeners to grasp. There is nothing so pathetic as hearing a speaker start a sentence and then lose the thread of it, so that he or she does not know how to finish it. It is a good plan for beginners especially to use only simple sentences, each consisting of subject, verb and predicate. Keep away from involved dependent clauses. Writing in short, staccato sentences may not be good style from a literary point of view – although it is better than writing over-involved sentences –

but it is the safest form of preparation for a speech. If you normally write in rather long sentences, split them up ruthlessly during revision. Remember that you have to say them – and breathe! Any faults of this kind that you make in the preparation will come back on you when you have to deliver the speech.

Do not use long words if you know shorter ones that mean the same thing. Do not say *commence* instead of *begin*, or *request* instead of *ask*, or *veracious* instead of *true*. The use of long words instead of short ones is not a sign of education and scholarship; it is a sign of ignorance. This is such a common fault that it is a good idea to devote one extra revision solely to the weeding out of words that can be replaced by shorter ones. The use of unnecessarily long words is a bad fault of style even in written English: in a speech it is inexcusable.

Similarly, do not seek uncommon words when you can say the same thing in words that are more familiar. It will only make your speech sound pompous and affected. Those of your audience who do not understand the words will be irritated, and those who do will think you are pretentious.

The best plan is to use words that you normally use in everyday conversation. If you are trying to use words that are not in your usual vocabulary, you run the risk of using them incorrectly, and if you do this your audience will laugh at you. Of course it is an advantage for a speaker to have a large vocabulary – but he or she should not keep one vocabulary for speeches and the other for day-to-day use.

The reason for all this is that above everything else you must try to be natural. Be yourself. If you don't the audience will soon spot your pose. Speak as you do in your everyday conversation. Do not think that because you are making a speech, you should use more 'refined' or 'educated' language. If you do, you merely show your lack of refinement and education.

## Archaisms and Clichés

The use of archaic and obsolete words is an affectation. The reason that words became archaic is that there is no longer any need for them. Usually they have been pushed out of the language by newcomers. You can never excuse yourself on the grounds that there is no other word to express your meaning: there always is.

Typical archaisms are *methinks, yclept, peradventure, whilom, behest, perchance, certes, anent* and *damsel*.

Equally important, and more difficult to observe is the necessity to avoid clichés. A cliché is usually an indirect way of expressing a simple idea which was probably striking when it was first used. However, frequent use, often in the wrong context, has left it banal and hackneyed and often meaningless. The strongest and most common objection to a cliché is simply that it is hackneyed.

The difficulty arises from the fact that clichés, like catch-phrases, are difficult to avoid. We read them in the newspaper, we hear them on the radio, and they are constantly used in normal conversation. Here you may argue that if a speech is to resemble conversation, then actually clichés ought to be permissible. The answer to this is that clichés are faults in all English, written and spoken, including conversation, and they are especially irritating when delivered in a public speech.

If you write out the first draft of your speech quickly – and you should do it quickly – then it will almost certainly contain several clichés. Never mind about them while you are writing, but go through the draft afterwards and weed them out.

Here are some typical clichés that should be avoided at all times: *the supreme sacrifice, the order of the day, a minus quantity, conspicuous by his absence, the devouring element* (i.e. fire), *slowly but surely, not wisely but too well, kindly but firmly, cruel to be kind, the cups that cheer but not inebriate, sleep the sleep of the just, what would be laughable if it were not tragic, has the defects of his qualities, the irony of fate, leave severely alone, more in sorrow than in anger,* and *the curate's egg.*

All these and many other similar expressions were neat or shrewd or witty when they were first used. They were pleasing because of their novelty. Now the novelty has worn off, and they are merely tedious. If you can think of an effective and original way of expressing something, use it. Then perhaps one day you will find it in a list of clichés.

# The Use of Slang

The use of slang depends to a great extent on the nature of your audience. It can be used to great effect, but it should always be used with a degree of restraint. It is, of course, entirely permissible in the relation of a humorous anecdote where it is called for. Similarly, on special subjects, such as sport, slang is almost a technical vocabulary, and is bound to be used. But do not use it for the sake of it. That is inverted snobbery as is the use of unnecessarily long or unfamiliar words. When in doubt, avoid slang.

Vulgarity should always be avoided. It may get a few cheap laughs, but it will not win over an audience. Avoid even the milder swear-words, such as *damned*. You don't gain anything by using them and you might cause offence to your audience. Similarly, avoid blasphemy.

## The Use of Quotations

Be careful about using quotations. An apt quotation can be very effective but it must be apt; and do not quote too much. The examples given after the specimen speeches and at the end of this book are for guidance only and should be used only if they really fit into what you are going to say. Never drag in a quotation just to show off your learning. Always avoid Latin and other foreign quotations. A deliberate show of education is the mark of an uneducated person.

You will note that few of the quotations given in this book are very familiar ones. They have been chosen carefully with this in mind. A hackneyed quotation is as bad as a cliché – indeed, many clichés are simply hackneyed quotations. Avoid those such as *To be or not to be, more honoured in the breach than in the observance*, etc.

Whenever you do use a quotation, make sure that you quote correctly. Do not use *A little knowledge is a dangerous thing* in error for *A little learning is a dangerous thing*, or *fresh fields and pastures new* in error for *fresh woods and pastures new*. Check your quotations before you use them.

## Humour

Some humour is desirable in most speeches and especially toasts, and in many it is absolutely necessary. There are several points to watch here. The first is that you must be sure that your jokes are in good taste. If you are at all doubtful that they might give offence, even if only to a few members of your audience, leave them out. The safest joke is a joke against yourself. The next point is that your humour must be amusing. An original joke is best, because then you can be sure that your audience will not have heard it before. Never repeat a joke you have heard on the radio, because that is bound to be well known. Keep clear of puns: they are not clever. Finally, your jokes must have some bearing on the subject of your speech. If a joke has been obviously dragged in it loses its point.

Humorous stories are valuable additions to most speeches, but they must observe the rules stated above. The biggest advantage with a humorous story is that it is easy to tell. It does not call for great oratory, and you are likely to find it easier to be natural when telling a tale than when speaking more formally. But, again, it must be in good taste, it must be new to the audience, and it must have sufficient bearing on your speech to justify its inclusion.

## Proposing a Toast

As is clear from the specimens in this book, many speeches made on social occasions are in the form of toasts or replies to toasts. All the hints given in this chapter apply equally to toasts as to other speeches, but when making a toast a few special factors need to be considered.

One is that the proposer of a toast has the advantage of not having to worry about how to end the speech. He or she simply invites the audience to drink, and the closing words are invariably the subject of the toast. This saves a lot of thought, because the ending of a speech is one of the two most difficult parts of it. The other difficult part, of course, is the beginning, and for this, in any social speech and especially in a toast, there is rarely anything better than a humorous reference or anecdote. It saves the speaker from the danger of being banal, it captures the interest and good humour of the audience at once, and because it is easy to relate it gives the speaker confidence in his or her ability to make the speech.

One more point must be considered in connection with toasts. You have been advised to be sincere in your speeches and not to say anything that you do not believe yourself. This holds good for toasts, too, although they always call for praise of the person or persons whose health is proposed. If you do not feel you can sincerely utter such a message, then try as tactfully as possible to decline to propose the toast. If you agree to toast a person whom you can praise with a clear conscience but of whom you are also critical you must, for the sake of courtesy, keep your criticism to yourself. But don't exaggerate the praise to make up for it! Exaggerated flattery is bound to be insincere, and audiences are quick to detect insincerity. Never write into your speech anything that you cannot honestly say with conviction.

## Last-minute Alterations to a Speech

When you prepare your speech you should always frame it in such a way that you can change it or add to it at the last minute – if necessary in the course of the function at which it is to be made.

This is very important. For one thing, it is possible you might be anticipated by a previous speaker saying something – perhaps telling a story – that is already down in your speech. You cannot say the same thing after him, so you must remove it from your speech and preserve continuity, if not length, by closing the gap. Another possible reason for having to make a last-minute alteration is a previous speaker saying something to which you will be expected to refer in your reply. You should not ignore this even if you could do so without making it obvious. Audiences are always favourably impressed when they hear something that the speaker could not possibly have thought out in advance.

A reply to a toast, of course, almost always involves last-minute changes and additions. However, such a speech should still be prepared in advance in the normal way, the only difference being that it should be made as general as possible. Usually you can anticipate the sort of things that will be said by the proposer of the toast, and your draft reply should answer these. But, of course, you must be ready to change your reply if the things you expect are not said, and you must be equally ready to answer any points made by the proposer that you have not anticipated. In this sense replying to a toast is extempore speaking, but that does not mean that the main part of the speech cannot be prepared in advance.

When you have to make an addition of this sort to your prepared speech, the best plan is to make it at the beginning. The audience will still have the point fresh in mind, and will be expecting you to reply – moreover will be delighted if you reply quickly, apparently without having had much time to think. But the main advantage to you is that you can deal with the addition at once, and can then get on with your prepared speech without having to worry about it any more.

## Good Grammar

Your speech should, of course, be grammatical. There are no special rules about grammar for speeches. In this respect the spoken word does not differ from the written word. You should speak as grammatically as you write, if you fail on grammar this has nothing to do with speech-making.

Still, a few points should be emphasised. The first is that being grammatical does not mean being pedantic. Good style, in writing as in speaking, is certainly grammatical, but excessive or misplaced regard for grammatical rules might ruin style altogether.

For example, at school you were probably taught that you should never end a sentence with a preposition. It is a sound rule, but sometimes it has to be broken. The alternative is to produce an ugly and ungainly sentence. This is bad in writing, and worse in speaking. Winston Churchill once ridiculed it brilliantly. He had to read a report prepared by a Civil Servant who had learnt the rule too thoroughly, and performed all sorts of verbal gymnastics to prevent prepositions from getting to the ends of his sentences. When Churchill had finished reading the report he wrote in the margin, 'This is the sort of English up with which I cannot put.'

Among the best books on grammar are H.W. Fowler's *Modern English Usage* and *The King's English*, both published by Oxford University Press, although you will find others in your local library or bookshop. Both those mentioned are entertaining reading as well as soundly instructive. Fowler had the highest standards but was broad-minded and tolerant to a degree unique for a grammarian. He pointed out, for example, that more bad English is written by those who try to avoid splitting infinitives (and yet do not really understand what a split infinitive is) than by those who regularly do so carelessly and cheerfully. You often see a needlessly ugly phrase such as *really to be understood*, obviously phrased in this ungainly fashion because the writer had the mistaken belief that *to be really understood* contained a split infinitive.

Fowler did not recommend splitting infinitives by any means, but he regarded the practice as a lesser evil than distorting sentences to escape from imaginary split infinitives. This is another example of the dangers of trying to be 'too grammatically correct'.

# Final Hints

When you prepare your speech always bear in mind that your principal object is to make your meaning clear, and the words you use must be chosen primarily for this purpose. The clearest way of saying a thing is usually the simplest. Avoid unnecessarily long words and circumlocutions. Do not say *I obtained not a little assistance from the arm of the law* when you mean *I got a lot of help from the constable*, or *We came to the parting of the ways*, when you mean *We parted*.

Never use two words when one will do. Always try for the maximum economy of language. Do not keep saying words such as *very* and *quite*. Wasting words takes up your time, obscures your meaning and irritates your audience.

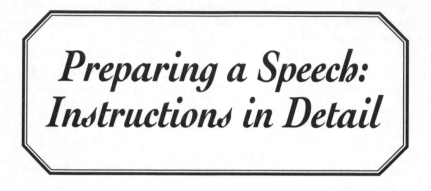

# CHAPTER TWO

# Preparing a Speech: Instructions in Detail

The last chapter contained general instructions on preparing speeches and toasts for all occasions. If you are only require to make a brief speech at a social gathering or to propose a toast, you will not need to do any further preparation. If, however, you are required to make a longer and more significant speech on a particular subject – for example, at a public meeting, or a meeting of a literary or similarly serious society, or as a principal in an organised debate – then more careful preparation will be necessary. It is for the preparation of a speech of the latter kind that this chapter has been written.

It was said in the last chapter that a speech is not an article, and that preparing something to be heard is a very different matter from preparing something to be read. This applies to every kind of speech, and it must be borne in mind throughout the preparations. You must never forget that your medium is to be the spoken and not the written word.

The secret of preparing a good speech on a definite subject is in the method. However good your ideas, unless you follow a method you will not be able to compose a coherent and effective speech. The same method can be used for all speeches, and once it has been mastered the work of preparation becomes quite straightforward.

To make the method clearer here, it will be applied to a

practical example. Let us suppose that you have to deliver a speech on the need for prison reform. (Even if you think that prisons do not need reform, that needn't influence your study of this chapter. This subject has been chosen as an example because it is fairly typical of the sort of speech delivered at public meetings, literary and debating societies, etc.)

# First Notes

Presumably you will already have some ideas on the subject, otherwise you would not have been asked, or you would not have agreed, to make the speech. So before you do anything else, jot down your ideas on a piece of paper. Let them come naturally – do not try to 'invent' any. There is no need to put them in any sort of order at this stage, but it is a good plan to put them under two headings, *Arguments* and *Facts*.

Regarding the arguments, you will see that this speech is of a partisan nature. It is to be one-sided. All speeches in debates, and most speeches at public and club meetings are one-sided. Only the chairman, who makes a brief summing up, is expected to be impartial. Your subject here is the *need* for prison reform, and you are expected to make a case. If the occasion for the speech is a debate, the opposing point of view will also be expressed. You must bear this in mind, and try to anticipate and disarm criticisms, and be careful not to say anything that will give your opponents an opportunity to gain debating points.

As you make your first notes, let your thoughts run freely, and you will find that one idea leads to another. Do not reject any idea because it does not seem to fit; selection will come later. Do not worry about how you are going to express your ideas, or the right words to use. Simply put everything down as it occurs to you, and go on in this way until you have run dry. Then put the piece of paper away and leave it for a day or so without thinking about it.

# Fleshing out your Notes

Now go back to your notes, and sort them. This means simply grouping the ideas together. You shouldn't try to put the groups into a definite order. Simply link up ideas that are of a similar nature. During this process you will find that fresh ideas will probably occur to you, so put these down as well. As before, do not try to force ideas if they are not already there.

Now make a note of the facts that need to be looked up or checked. For this purpose you will need encyclopedias or other reference books, most of which you will probably be able to find in your local library. The wisest plan is to check every fact you can. In a debate especially, it is vital that you should not make any error of fact, even of detail. An otherwise excellent speech can be utterly ruined by a factual mistake. If you are in doubt about a fact, and cannot check it properly, leave it out.

Next test the validity of your arguments. Ask yourself if they are really convincing. If they don't convince you, it is unlikely that they will convince your audience. If your speech includes only one unconvincing argument, the audience will be more sceptical about your sound arguments.

Now consider whether your knowledge of the subject is really adequate. On a subject such as prison reform you will help yourself a great deal if you can obtain permission to visit a prison. Then you will be able to speak with first-hand authority, and of course the visit itself will certainly give you fresh ideas. On this subject, too, you ought to read reports of Royal Commissions and similar documents. There is lots of literature on the subject, and you should read as many as you can. You mustn't copy from the books of others, however. It is your speech, and it will not be a good one unless it expresses your views. That is why you have been advised to write down your own ideas before delving into relevant literature.

A large part of the reading should be of books by opponents of prison reform. Study their arguments, and try to find answers to them. If you are speaking in a debate, you may be sure that opposing arguments that have already been published will be repeated by your opponents. Be ready for them. Anticipate them and 'kill'; them before they are uttered.

It will be a good idea to seek information about books and other sources of material from a society that is devoted to the subject on which you are to speak. Thus for prison reform you could approach the Howard League for Penal Reform. You will find the address of this and other similar societies in *Whitaker's Almanack*. But do not do this until you have first put down your own ideas.

When you have gathered all your material – that is, ideas from your brain and facts from reference sources – the time has come for you to compose the framework of your speech. Generally speaking, a speech consists of three parts: the beginning or pre-oration; the middle, or discussion; and the end, or peroration.

# Pre-oration

The importance of the pre-oration is that it should capture the attention of the audience. Avoid saying anything banal or obvious. For example *The prisons in this country are in grave need of reform* would be a weak opening sentence.

On a social occasion, or when the speech is of a light character, it is a good idea to begin with a touch of humour. If, for example, you were speaking in a debate on whether men were better cooks than women, you could start with a personal domestic anecdote. In a speech on a subject like prison reform, however, a humorous opening would be out of place, so you must think of a different sort of introduction.

A topical reference is often a good solution to this problem. Look through the newspapers, and pick out a court case that has aroused general public interest. Let us suppose that a burglar named John Smith, aged 21, has been sent to prison for three years. Now take a piece of paper and write down:

## 1. Introduction

John Smith, burglar, 21. Three years.

Your subject is prison, and you have got to get on to this theme at once. The case of John Smith makes this easy. You have brought home to your audience the reality of crime and now you are going to bring home to them the reality of prisons. You do this by asking them if they have any idea of where, and to what, John Smith is going? What is in store for him during the next three years? So you write down, still under the same heading (1):

Where is he going?

Now you enlarge on this from you original list of notes. This is where a personal visit to a prison will be of great help to you. Failing that, you must take facts obtained from reference books, reports of Royal Commissions, etc. This part of the speech should be brief, but it must be vivid. Do not exaggerate. Do not even express any opinion yet. In this part of the speech you need only facts.

So conclude this section with the note:

Personal visit (or report of Royal Commission, etc.).

# Middle Discussion

The middle part of a speech can be divided roughly into four parts which may be summarised under the following headings:

Statement of the proposition or argument that you wish to prove.
The evidence in detail.
The summary of evidence.
Exposition of the conclusion logically to be drawn from such evidence.

These headings will, of course, want sub-divisions. The evidence in detail will occupy a large part of your speech, and will need to be split up into several parts.

## *Proposition or Argument*

You want to prove something – in this case that prisons need reform. (That is implicit in the title of your speech.) Therefore you must say first of all why they need reform. You must say what, in your opinion, is wrong with them.

You will find your material in your original notes, under the heading *Arguments*. Select them carefully, leaving out anything that seems weaker or less relevant to the question. Arrange them in order, and then make notes of the salient points. Let us suppose for the sake of the illustration that you consider that the main thing wrong with prisons is that they are out of date. Society's attitude to criminals has changed, but parallel changes in prison buildings and, to some extent, the whole system, have lagged behind. Most prisons were built in the days when it was generally accepted that the punishment should fit the crime. Now society considers in general that the punishment should fit the criminal. The prisons were built before the idea of reformation and rehabilitation of prisoners was accepted, and the prison administration, while greatly improved, still needs reform.

So in this section you would write:

Prisons need reform.
Punishment fit the criminal, not the crime.
Buildings no longer suitable.
Administration needs modernisation.

## *Evidence in Detail*

Now move on to the evidence in detail. Its quantity will be governed by the amount of time you are allowed for your speech. Certainly you will have to select ruthlessly, and even the facts that are included will have to be compressed. Naturally you will want to include as many facts as possible, but don't try to include everything if this means you will not be able to do anything justice. It is better to leave out the less impressive facts and make the most of the strongest ones. Don't hesitate to weed out anything that is not strictly relevant or that does not fit in with its neighbours. There must be no suspicion of digression in your speech. It must be arranged in a logical and orderly manner, with each point leading naturally on to the next.

The evidence, of course, comes from your original notes under the heading *Facts*. Take what you need and arrange it in the most suitable order. Then write down your notes. They might be something like this:

Physical overcrowding.
Poor hygiene and sanitation.
More open prisons needed.
Stultifying influence of unnecessary petty restrictions.
Inadequate provision of useful employment.
Lack of proper educational facilities.
Insufficient classification and segregation of prisoners.
Insufficient constructive reformatory work.

## Summary of Evidence

This section will be much briefer. For example:

Overcrowding and bad conditions.
Repressive influence.
Insufficient rehabilitation.

## *Logical Conclusions*

The conclusions you draw from all the above form the most important part of your speech, and must be clear and forceful. They must also anticipate possible criticisms of your arguments and, if possible, disarm them. One obvious criticism is lack of finance, and you might answer this in advance by pointing out that unless conditions are changed there will be more 'chronic' criminals and that crime costs the nation more than the reforms would. That is to say, far from not being able to afford to make reforms, we cannot afford *not* to make them.

You should also bring out the most constructive features of your argument. In this particular example, of course, there is constructive criticism from the beginning of the speech, but in general the way to present an argument is to criticise the present state of affairs, first pointing out the things that are wrong, and then saying how they could be made better.

Bearing these points in mind, you could summarise your logical conclusions as follows:

System out of date.
Theory not put into practice.
Need for new buildings and better administration.
Cannot afford not to reform prisons.

# Peroration

Finally comes your peroration, and this is perhaps the most difficult part of your speech. Like the pre-oration, it should be striking, but in a different way: your object is to leave something in your listeners' ears – something that they will continue to remember after you have sat down. A really apt quotation makes a good peroration. Failing that, try to end with a trenchant epigram or a paradox.

In this case a possible theme for the peroration is a denial of sentimentality. Prison reformers are often labelled by their opponents as well-meaning but unrealistic people who do not understand the harsh facts of crime. You can anticipate this criticism and at the same time startle your listeners by declaring bluntly that you have no time for sentiment in this matter, and demand that they look at it from a strictly practical point of view. Returning indirectly to the financial angle, ask them if we can afford to allow crime to continue at its present high level. Say bluntly that there are only two ways of preventing criminals from returning to crime. One is to execute them, or at least keep them in prison until they die; the other is to reform them. At present a fatal middle course is being pursued. Modern society would not allow the extermination of all criminals, and therefore the only sane course is to try to reform them. Put the notes for the peroration as follows:

No time for sentiment.
Exterminate or reform.

# Pattern of your Speech

Now you have the whole pattern of your speech. Your notes will read as follows:

**1. Pre-oration or introduction**
John Smith, burglar, 21. Three years.
Where is he going?
Personal visit (or report of Royal Commission, etc.).

**2. Proposition or argument**
Prisons need reform.
Punishment fit the criminal, not the crime.
Buildings no longer suitable.
Administration needs modernisation.

**3. Evidence in detail**
Physical overcrowding.
Poor hygiene and sanitation.
More open prisons needed.
Stultifying influence of unnecessary petty restrictions.
Inadequate provision of useful employment.
Lack of proper educational facilities.
Insufficient classification and segregation of prisoners.
Insufficient constructive reformatory work.

**4. Summary of evidence**
Overcrowding and bad conditions.
Repressive influences.
Insufficient rehabilitation.

**5. Logical conclusions**
System out of date.
Theory not yet put into practice.
Need for new buildings and better administration.
Cannot afford not to reform prisons.

**6. Peroration, or conclusion**
No time for sentiment.
Exterminate or reform.

# Abridged Notes

Before you go any further, try to reduce these to a more compact form. Put them into a kind of private shorthand, to which you alone hold the key, trying to compress ideas into single words which will be sufficient to remind you of the longer notes. For example:

1. John Smith, 21, 3 years. Where going? Visit.
2. Reform. Punishment fit criminal. Buildings unsuitable.

Administration.
3. Overcrowding. Hygiene. Open prisons. Restrictions. Employment. Education. Classification. Constructive work.
4. Overcrowding. Repression. Rehabilitation.
5. Out of date. Theory-practice. Buildings, administration. Cannot afford.
6. Sentiment. Exterminate or reform.

The purpose of this abridged set of notes will be explained in the next chapter.

## Finalising the Framework of your Speech

Now return to the longer notes, number (1) to (6). This is the framework of your speech, so before you go any further read the notes again as critically as you can, and ask yourself:

● Do they include anything that does not fit in or that could be omitted without weakening the argument?

● Is there any repetition or bad arrangement that is likely to cause the speech to be longer than it need be?

● Is the existing arrangement logical and orderly, so that each idea naturally leads to the next?

● Does this arrangement of your ideas really represent what you want to say?

Next turn to your original notes and read through the facts and arguments that were not selected for inclusion. If any of these seems too important to be left out, consult the framework again to see if you can modify it to include the omitted matter.

## Writing your Speech

The next step is to write out your speech. Do this quickly without bothering to spend minutes on trying to find the best words. Speak it aloud as you write it, but do not try to revise as you go along. Do not ramble away from your headings. If you get new ideas, put them down on a separate piece of paper, for consideration after the rough draft is finished.

When your speech is finished, read it through aloud once. Then settle down to revise it. You cannot spend too much time on this. You should polish it, rephrase it, and constantly try to improve it in every possible way. Be highly critical of it. If a word does not seem quite right, try to find a better one. You will find synonyms in any dictionary and many more in *Roget's Thesaurus*. Consider each argument, and see if you can find a clearer and more forceful way of expressing the points you want to make.

When at last your revision is complete put the speech away for a day or so. Then get it out and again read it aloud, and make any further revisions that seem necessary. There will always be some!

Now time the speech, allowing for pauses. If it is too long, cut it ruthlessly. Don't keep telling yourself that if you cut it down you will not do justice to your subject. Remember that you will have left your strongest arguments to the end, and they are not going to have much effect if half your audience is asleep before they are delivered.

When you have got your speech down to the allotted length – a little less is better than a little more – polish it again. You can go on polishing at intervals right up until the time has come for you to make the speech, and after each revision it will look more and more like a finished speech.

Finally, take out your set of abridged notes and compare them with the speech. Modify them to take into account the revisions you have made. This check will serve the additional purpose of showing whether you have kept to the logical and orderly arrangement of your ideas.

The next step is to prepare for the delivery.

# CHAPTER THREE

# Delivering a Speech

I t has been said that the best advice on making a speech is embodied in the simple injunction to stand up, speak up and shut up. The question of shutting up has already been dealt with in the remarks in Chapter 1 on the necessity for brevity. This chapter will deal with the equally important matters of standing up and speaking up.

Before the actual delivery is discussed, however, a few words must be said about memorising the speech. It has been shown how each speech should be prepared and written out beforehand. The next step is to turn it into the spoken word.

## Memorising the Speech

There are four ways of learning a speech. It can be read, it can be learnt by heart and recited, it can be memorised more broadly but not delivered word for word, or it can be so memorised that the speaker will, with the aid of a few notes, be able to deliver it nearly in the form in which it was prepared.

Reading a speech is the worst method, and it should be avoided. It has many disadvantages. The main one, of course is that it never sounds really convincing, and the audience is unsympathetic from the beginning. There is the well-known case of the speaker who stood up, solemnly produced a sheaf of papers from his pocket, adjusted his glasses and began to read: 'It is with considerable surprise that I see so many faces of old friends before me.' Of course the old friends laughed – but only because he was reading it and thus giving away that he had written those words before he knew how many old friends would be there. Another disadvantage of reading a speech is that the speaker does not allow himself the opportunity of modifying his speech in the light of what has been said by previous speakers. The necessity for this was mentioned in Chapter 2.

This latter disadvantage applies equally to learning by heart and then reciting. This is not as bad as reading, but is hardly to be recommended. Unless the speaker is naturally a brilliant actor, the speech will probably sound flat and artificial. There is a further danger. There is no prompter, and if an attack of nerves causes the speaker to lose their place, utter confusion and probably panic will result.

The third method is excellent for the practised speaker but hardly recommended for the beginner. It involves a heavy strain on the memory, and adroitness in the use of words.

The fourth method is probably the most suitable for all but accomplished speakers. The work of memorising the speech is done automatically in the preparation, and in the case of a long speech the notes will simply be the abridged notes referred to in Chapter 2. You might be dismayed at the thought of not repeating every word of the speech that you took so much trouble to prepare, write and revise, but you can take comfort from the fact that your memory will almost certainly prove an excellent sieve, retaining the best things and rejecting the worthless.

Your author had a lesson in the value of this sieve early in his career as a public speaker. By chance he had been asked by two societies to speak on the same subject within a matter of a few days. Rather unwisely, he prepared exactly the same speech for both occasions, although he knew the audiences were unalike. His wife (who was present on both occasions) noticed that the two speeches as delivered differed from each other in many particulars. Afterwards he and his wife went over the original draft of the speech and made an illuminating discovery. The memory had acted as a censor as well as a sieve, having done what the speaker himself ought to have done in preparing the speeches; it had rejected different things on the two occasions, according to the unsuitability for the respective audiences.

Where this fourth method of memorising the speech is used, the notes should be written – or, better, typed – on a postcard. They must be clear enough for you to read merely by glancing down. Unless you are short-sighted, do not hold the card while delivering the speech, but simply place it on the table in front of you. Consult it with the smallest possible ostentation, preferable during enforced pauses for cheers or laughter. A quick glance down should be enough to assure you of the next point on your speech.

Good delivery can come only with practice, and the best practice is to take your card of notes into an empty room and address an imaginary audience. Having decided not to learn the speech by heart and then recite it, do not keep breaking off while you search your memory for the exact words you wrote. You must be prepared to sacrifice these. Don't think that you wasted your time taking so much trouble to compose your speech. Had you not written it out in full and constantly revised it, you would find it much harder to acquire fluency.

That, of course, is another reason why this method is preferable both to reading and learning by heart. However hard you may have tried to bear in mind that you were composing a speech and not writing an article, you will almost certainly have included a few sentences that are expressed more in the manner of the written than the spoken word. Your memory censor will come to your help here by rejecting purely literary expressions and forcing you to substitute expressions suitable for oratory. This will help greatly to make the speech sound more natural.

That you should try to make the speech sound natural is another way of saying that you should try to persuade your audience that it was not prepared beforehand! The aim of good delivery is to deceive. Firstly you prepared your speech with great care. Now, in delivery it, you use all your ability to make it sound spontaneous. If the speech were read this would be impossible, and if it were learnt by heart and then recited it would be very difficult.

While you are practising your delivery of the speech with the aid of your notes, you will probably find that, in spite of all your careful revision, it still contains some things that sound stilted, and more suitable expressions will occur to you. Adopt them; don't think that just because your speech has been beautifully written out or typed that it should not be touched. It is never too late to improve – and in the matter of speaking, your tongue is always wiser than your pen.

You might find it helpful to try out your speech on a member of your family or a friend. This practice can be useful, but there are dangers in it. You will almost certainly get some criticism, and you must be careful how far you accept it. Consider first if your experimental audience is of the same type as the audience for which your speech has been composed. For example, a maiden aunt is not the best person to given an opinion on a speech made for an old boys' dinner. Then bear in mind that there is a tremendous difference between the effect of a speech on a single listener who knows you intimately and its effect on an audience of two or three hundred who do not know you nearly so well. A humorous reference or a joke may fall flat in rehearsal, and yet be greeted with a lot of laughter when it comes to the actual delivery. Remember that it is always easier to amuse many people together than one individual. Even a feeble joke can cause amusement if there are enough people hearing it together. That is why radio comedians like to have a studio audience.

## Stage Fright

Now we come to the actual delivery, the standing up and speaking up. Your first difficulty, at least in your maiden speech, will probably be in controlling your nerves. You will be afflicted with what actors call stage fright.

Overcoming stage fright is solely a matter of confidence, and therefore the first lesson you must learn is that it *can be* overcome. It will help you if you realise that it is a universal affliction of speakers, and not peculiar to you. Remember that the most eloquent speakers you hear now were probably very nervous when they first began to speak in public.

There is only one certain way of overcoming nervousness, and that is simply practice. This is why it is such a good idea to join a debating society prior to public speaking. Failing this, practise by yourself either in an empty room or to the rest of your family – if they'll let you! But whenever you practise do it properly. Make it a dress rehearsal, and try to imagine that you are addressing a real audience. Otherwise it will be of little help. Practise with the speech you have prepared, and with some of the specimens in the book. To begin with you can simply read these aloud; then try to delivery similar speeches without the book.

When the time comes for you to deliver your speech, you will probably find this simple little exercise helpful. Just before you are about to rise, deflate your lungs and then take in a full breath of air and expel it slowly. Do this two or three times. It will increase the supply of oxygen to your blood, and thus steady your nerves.

Finally, be careful of seeking Dutch courage at the bar. A drink may bolster up your confidence temporarily, but too much alcohol will certainly be disastrous. It will ruin your delivery, and cloud your brain at a time when it should be at its sharpest.

As nerves are felt most at the beginning of a speech, you should have considered this matter in preparing your pre-oration. There is no point in starting with a brilliant sentence if you do not feel you are capable of delivering it properly. A humorous allusion or anecdote is always a good beginning for the novice, because it is the easiest to relate. Automatically you slip into a natural, conversational style, and the battle of nerves is won.

## Standing Up

Every public speaker must know how to stand properly. But before you stand you have to rise, and the importance of the way you do this is rarely considered. In fact it is very important indeed.

When you are called upon to get up, you might feel slightly sick, you want to avoid the gaze of the audience and your legs seem flabby. Unless you get a grip on yourself you will probably get up slowly and reluctantly, and begin with your knees still bent, while your feet are shuffling on the floor.

That is no good at all. Get a grip on yourself at once, stand up smartly, and face your audience squarely. If you do this you will find that your nerves are much better than they were a few seconds earlier. There is nothing like a show of confidence, even if it is bravado, to make you feel confident.

Your standing position should be easy and comfortable. The first rule is simple: don't pose. Don't try to stand like a soldier on parade. Place your feet apart and put yourself at ease.

Don't loll in a slovenly fashion. Stand upright and don't begin speaking until you have completed the process of standing up. A momentary pause should be made before the speech is begun. It is better to put the weight of your body on one foot rather than on both. For one thing it is less tiring; for another, it enables you to turn from one side to the other. But that is not to say that you should be constantly swaying when you are speaking. On the contrary, you should keep your body as still as possible. Above all, keep your feet still.

The position of your head is most important. You will notice that at most public meetings the speaker stands on a raised platform, so that he or she looks slightly down on the audience. One reason for this is that it is easier to speak if the head is tilted forward and downwards a little. If it is held too high the muscles of the throat will be restricted.

Your hands will probably worry you at first. They will seem enormous and you won't know what to do with them. There are several things that you should *not* do. Don't let them hang limply by your sides, or you will feel – and look – ill at ease. Don't fold them across your chest, or you won't be able to breathe properly. Don't try to rest them on the table in front of you, as this will probably be too low, and so you will have to bend forward all the time.

There are four places to put your hands. You can grasp the lapels of your jacket, although this is not recommended; it makes you want to fidget nervously. A better place is the back of a chair or the rail of the platform in front of you. This will be at the proper height and having something to grasp will increase your confidence. A safe place is behind your back. The fourth possibility is in your pockets, and on an informal occasion this is as good as any. But if you decide to put your hands in your pockets, keep them there, and don't jingle keys or money or you will irritate your audience.

The position of your hands, like everything else, is a problem that disappears after practice. The experienced speaker doesn't think about his or her hands and they naturally fall into a suitable place.

The matter of gesticulation is simple. First of all, never invent a gesture. Don't make a deliberate movement of your hands or arms in an attempt to give emphasis to your words. It will make you look like a clown. Therefore don't think about gestures at all, until they come of their own accord. You will find, as you warm to your subject, that you are making spontaneous gestures. These are natural, so don't attempt to alter them. Let them come. The only time you need to interfere is when they are coming too frequently. Remember that the British as a nation do not like a lot of demonstrativeness and if you find that your hands and arms are moving about too much, you must control them.

Finally, consider your eyes. Don't look at the floor. Don't look at the ceiling. Look at the audience, and at the back of the audience for preference. If you are speaking from notes, learn to take them in with an occasional quick glance downwards, preferably during a pause.

## Correct Breathing

Speaking, like singing, requires correct breathing. The first rule is simply that you should throw out your chest. In other words, take as much air into your lungs as you can, and never exhaust them completely. Keeping your shoulders back and your abdomen drawn in slightly will help you to do this. Breathe in more air at every opportunity. Inhale only through the nose if you can. It is important that the taking of a breath should be accomplished in silence. If you are speaking into a microphone this is essential.

Give yourself plenty of opportunity for taking in fresh breaths. Do not attempt to deliver too many words without a pause, or you will find that you are forced to make an unintended pause simply to take in more air. This can spoil the effect of your speech.

## Speaking Up

It almost goes without saying that a speech should be audible, yet inaudibility is one of the commonest errors in public speaking. It is also the least excusable, because speaking up is quite simple even for those without naturally powerful voices.

Speak clearly, and open your mouth. Don't mumble. Don't fall into the common fault of dropping your voice at the end of sentences. Aim at the back of your audience. There is no need to shout to make your voice carry. Do not speak too rapidly. If you are interrupted by applause or laughter, wait until silence has returned before going on. The same applies to other interruptions. If members of your audience are ill-mannered enough to whisper while you are speaking, do not glare at them. Simply pause, and they will soon stop whispering. The same applies if there is a noise of plate and glass or particularly loud aircraft or traffic outside.

During practice you will have divided your speech up into phrases, with pauses between them. You will have found from experience that 'punctuation' in speaking is not the same as writing. You have to make many additional pauses where there are no commas. These pauses should be made intelligently, however. A good pause can be more effective than words. Also, pauses should be of different lengths. Generally speaking, the more important the words that *follow* the pause, the longer the pause should be. Take these pauses seriously, because they are a vital part of your speech. Fit your breathing to the pauses, not the pauses to your breathing.

Here is an example of the correct use of pauses. It is the famous tribute made by Winston Churchill to the RAF during the Second World War. The sentence reads:

*Never in the field of human conflict was so much owed by so many to so few.*

It will be seen that this sentence does not contain a single comma or other punctuation mark until the full stop at the end. Yet if it were spoken without any pauses it would lose all its effectiveness.

Divide the sentence as follows:

*Never* – very short pause – *in the field of human conflict* – short pause – *was so much* – short pause – *owed by so many* – longer pause – *to so few.*

Not all these pauses are necessary for breathing but they are all needed to give the words the full significance that they deserve. Notice that the longest pause comes before the most important words – *to so few.*

Closely linked with the subject of pauses is the use of emphasis. Again, there is a big difference between the written and the spoken word. When a writer wants to emphasise a word or phrase, he or she puts it in *italics*. Good writers use italics very sparingly. In speaking, however, 'verbal italics' are necessary on a much bigger scale.

For example, take this simple sentence: It can be done; it will be done. In writing this, no italics are needed. But if it is spoken, the verbs must be emphasised, so that it becomes: It *can* be done; it *will* be done. Emphasis, like the pause, should be varied. Don't over-emphasise everything or your emphasis will lose its value, and you will have nothing left for really important words. Your emphasis should range from light to heavy, and should be used with care.

## Manner of Speaking

Your manner of speech will depend very much on the occasion and the audience. However, certain general principles apply to all circumstances.

Don't be pompous or patronising. You must win over the audience. Don't talk down. On the other hand, don't try to be over-familiar, or you might appear vulgar.

Vary your tone according to the subject matter of your speech. Avoid monotony of delivery. Modulate your tones. Be sincere. Put all the meaning you can into your words, but don't be theatrical. Whatever else your manner is, it must be natural. It should be a polished version of your normal conversational manner. Even if the members of the audience don't know you, they will be quick to sense artificiality of manner, and the reception of your speech will suffer accordingly.

Don't punctuate your speech with *ums* and *ahs*. You may not realise it yourself, but they are very irritating, and it can become a habit that is increasingly difficult to cure. The chief cause of this fault is, of course, insufficient preparation of the speech. The other main cause is lack of concentration. The speaker says *um* or *ah* to gain time while thinking what to say next. If you must pause to think, then let it be a silent pause.

## Elocution and Articulation

It was said earlier in this chapter that you don't need to have a powerful voice to make yourself audible. It isn't volume that makes it possible for your audience to hear what you are saying. It is, rather, the way you say it.

Speaking is a manner of communication, and correct speaking is nothing more than clear speaking. Many snobbish comments have been made about accents, and this can be disposed of very briefly. If you have a Scottish or Yorkshire or any other accent, don't try to conceal it. It gives character to your delivery. The only thing you have to watch is that it should not prevent your audience from understanding what you are saying.

So use your natural accent. Don't try to adopt, for example, an Oxford accent in the mistaken belief that it is more refined. This will be an affectation, and you will neither convince nor please your audience.

Whatever your accent, you must make sure that you pronounce your words clearly and distinctly. The commonest error in elocution is failure to pronounce certain letters.

Slackness over the letter *h* is well known, for example, dropping the initial *h* is its commonest form, as in words such as house (*'ouse*) and holiday (*'oliday*). The reverse of the error is to put an *h* where it doesn't belong as in ambition (*hambition*) and especially in words beginning with an *h* mute such as heir, honest and hour. These twin faults can often be avoided by care over the pronunciation of the definite article (the). When this comes before a vowel or *h* mute it should be pronounced *thee*; when before a consonant, it should be pronounced simply *th* with a short vowel sound to separate it from the first letter of the following word. If this rule is observed it becomes almost physically impossible to go wrong.

A more common fault is ignoring the letter *h* in words such as what, when and where. Yet another common error is to run on words like *is he* into something that sounds like *izzee*.

The first rule in elocution is that each word should be spoken separately, and that all the letters that are meant to be pronounced are pronounced. This may involve making a brief pause between words, but the gain in clearness and distinctness is immeasurable. Letters that often get lost are final *ds* and *ts* and *ks* and the *g* in words ending in *ing*. To say *that time* or *and did* correctly involves a definite pause between words. In practising this you may find at first that it sounds stilted and awkward, but with further practice you will eventually find it just as easy to pronounce the words correctly as incorrectly.

The pronunciation of the final *r* depends on whether a vowel begins the next word. In the expression *weather bulletin*, for example, the *r* at the end of weather is barely pronounced but if you say *tar and feather* you must pronounce the *r* in tar distinctly. You must not, of course, put in an *r* to join a word ending with a vowel to a word beginning a vowel, as in the *idea of* (the idear of) or *I saw an engine* (I sawr an engine). This error is just as bad as putting in an *h* where it doesn't belong.

All these errors can be avoided if you practise saying each word slowly and distinctly, and pronouncing every letter that is not mute. It is a good plan to practise speaking before a looking glass, to make sure that you are using your lips, teeth and tongue in the proper way. Bad vowel sounds are usually the result of failure to open the mouth properly; slackness over the letters *t* and *d* is caused by failure to bring the tongue in proper relation to the teeth.

Most dictionaries give pronunciation as well as definitions, and whenever you are in doubt you should check these. A common error is putting the wrong stress on a word, and you will find that usually the mistake is in putting the stress on the second syllable when it ought to be on the first. Examples are ca*pit*alist in error for *cap*italist, ap*plic*able for *ap*plicable; com*par*able in error for *com*parable, mis*chie*vous in error for *mis*chievous and re*mon*strate in error for *rem*onstrate.

Other errors in pronunciation are the simple result of errors in spelling, usually accompanied by a misunderstanding of the meanings of words. Your dictionary will tell you, for example, the differences between *complaisant* and *complacent*, *palatial* and *palatal*, *allusion* and *illusion*, *perspicacity* and *perspicuity*, *mendacity* and *mendicity*, *fermentation* and *fomentation*, *ingenious* and *ingenuous*, and many others.

The most common errors are made in long or relatively uncommon words. This is yet another argument in favour of using short and simple words. There is, for example, no reason why you should ever use either mendacity or mendicity. The former means lying and the latter means begging, and you cannot do better than use the simpler words.

# Audience Reaction and Heckling

A speech is made by one person and heard by others, but the processes of speaking and hearing are very closely linked. In a good ˙speech, the speaker and the audience are in harmony, and the task of obtaining this balance rests with the speaker.

When you prepare your speech you should consider what sort of audience you can expect, and try to compose something that will appeal to them. However, not even the most experienced speaker can gauge exactly how the audience will react to what he or she has to say. Therefore, while you are speaking, observe what effect your words are having, and be ready to modify your speech accordingly as you go on.

Suppose, for example, that you have brought in a witty reference to some institution, and it has fallen very flat. This might be because it is not as witty as you thought it was. Alternatively, it might be because this particular audience doesn't appreciate or even dislikes this sort of witticism. Now suppose that you have a similar witticism later in the speech, and you have a strong feeling that it is going to be equally poorly received. There is only one thing to do: cut it out.

Again you will be able to tell from the reaction of your audience whether the speech is going well generally. Yawns and whispers and half-hearted laughs and tepid applause all add up to boredom. There is only one answer to this: cut your speech short. Finish it off as quickly as you can, and sit down. Even if you do this abruptly, the effect will not be bad; on the contrary, the audience will probably now think that your speech was actually better than it seemed. You will at least have obliged them by saving them from the amount of boredom they were beginning to expect. Don't make the mistake of thinking that your listeners will get less bored as you go on. They will get more bored, unless the latter part of your speech is very different from the first part.

Heckling is rarely experienced outside political meetings, and it requires a ready wit to be put down effectively. If you are heckled, keep cool and don't lose your temper. The hecklers are trying to rile you, and if they succeed you will have no peace until you sit down.

The best weapon against heckling is quick wit. Without being spiteful or malicious, try to get the audience to laugh with you at the expense of the heckler. Although the hecklers make the most noise, they are usually only a small minority of the audience.

An example of brilliant repartee was given by George Bernard Shaw when he made the curtain speech on the first night of one of his plays. The final curtain was the signal for applause and cries of 'Author!' When Shaw appeared, the audience further showed its approval by applauding still more loudly. Then, as the clapping and cheering died down, a single but very loud boo came down from the gallery. Shaw looked up and said, 'I quite agree with you, sir – but what are we two against so many who hold a different opinion?'

## Hamlet's Advice

Public speaking, as has been stressed more than once, is very different from acting; but much of the advice given by Hamlet to the players can well be taken to heart by the person who has to make a speech. Hamlet said,

*'Speak the speech, I pray you,*
*as I pronounc'd it to you, trippingly on the tongue;*
*but if you mouth it, as many of our players do,*
*I had as lief the town-crier spoke my lines.*
*Nor do not saw the air too much with your hand, thus,*
    *but use all gently;*
*for in the very torrent, tempest, and, as I may say,*
*the whirlwind of passion,*
*you must acquire and beget*
*a temperance that may give it smoothness ...*
*Be not too tame neither,*
*but let your own discretion be your tutor.*
*Suit the action to the word, the word to the action;*
*with this special observance,*
*that you o'erstep not the modesty of nature.'*

# CHAPTER FOUR

# Duties of the Chair

The proceedings of meetings and functions of all kinds are invariably controlled by a chairperson, who is elected or appointed for this purpose.

A chairperson should be an individual with a strong personality, capable of keeping order, genial and even-tempered, a fairly able speaker who knows when to stop, and – perhaps most important of all – a person of tact.

The duties of the chair vary considerably according to the nature of the meeting or function. For convenience this chapter is divided into three sections, explaining the duties of the chair at a meeting of a club or society, at a public meeting, and at a social dinner or other function. The chair's duties at a company meeting lie outside the scope of this book.

## At a Meeting of a Club or Society

The chairperson's first duty is normally to have the minutes of the last meeting read, usually by the club secretary. When the minutes have been read, it will be formally moved that the minutes be approved. This motion is usually carried unanimously, but it is possible that a member of the meeting will question their accuracy or raise a point of issue. The chairperson must allow discussion of this, but must be careful also to ensure that speakers keep strictly to the subject. A question on the minutes is sometimes used as an excuse for general discussion, and anything of this nature must be ruled out of order.

If an alteration in the minutes is agreed upon, it must be made as an amendment. The secretary will insert it in its proper place and initial it.

When the meeting has formally approved the minutes the chairperson will sign them, and then turn to the main business of the meeting. This may have been set out as an agenda. If so, the chair will take the first point and continue until the whole agenda has been covered.

As each subject is introduced for discussion, the chair has the privilege of speaking first. However, as it is part of the duty of the chair to be impartial, remarks should be confined to statements of the facts and issues. In any case, comments should be brief and to the point in order to set an example to other speakers.

When a formal resolution is moved, the proposer naturally speaks first and is followed by the seconder. There is no fixed order of speakers in the general discussion. Each person who wants to speak has to catch the chairperson's eye, and it is the duty of the chair to ensure that everyone who wishes to speak has the opportunity to do so. It might be necessary to curtail lengthy speeches, especially when the speaker strays from the subject, and this is where there is the need for tact. The chairperson should always try persuasion rather than enforcement of authority.

The proposer of a motion has the right to speak a second time when all the other speakers have given their views. Then the question is put to the vote. This is usually recorded by a show of hands. Under the rules of most clubs and societies, if there is an equal division of votes for and against the motion the chair has the casting vote.

Any amendment to a motion must be voted on before the motion itself.

When the vote has been taken, the chairperson announces whether the motion is carried or not, and introduces the next item of business.

When the business of the meting has been concluded, the chairperson declares the meeting closed.

# At a Public Meeting

The duties of the chair of a public meeting, for example a political meeting, are quite simple. He or she merely introduces the speakers, usually with a few pleasant personal remarks.

At a party political meeting, of course, the chairperson is not expected to pretend to be impartial. However, he or she should leave controversial questions to the principal speaker or speakers, and refrain from making a long speech. See Chapter 9 Political and Electoral for examples.

# At a Social Dinner or Other Function

At social gatherings the chairperson's functions are quite different. At a dinner the first duty is to propose the toast of the Queen (see Chapter 5 Loyal and Patriotic Toasts).

It should be noted in the specimen speeches that there are many other toasts usually proposed by the chair. The speech for proposing such toasts is made in the same way as similar speeches by others.

Otherwise the chairperson has only to call upon the other speakers, whose names and toasts will have been decided in advance. No speech of introduction is needed here. It is sufficient simply to say, 'I now call upon — to propose the toast of ...'. When the toast has been proposed and drunk the chairperson calls upon the responder in the same way. It is best to finish the business of eating first, and then when everybody has relaxed and is sitting back with coffee and liqueurs to have all the toasts and speeches at one go.

When there is a musical or other entertainment, the chairperson introduces each item in turn.

# CHAPTER FIVE

# Loyal and Patriotic Toasts

## The Queen

This toast is usually proposed by the chairperson or host. It always heads the toast list. Smoking is not permitted until this toast has been given, so the chair is expected to propose it as soon as possible after the last course of the meal has been finished. The proposer is not required to make a speech. He simply rises and utters the time-honoured formula:

Ladies and gentlemen – the Queen!

Immediately after this toast the chairperson should announce:

Ladies and gentlemen, you may smoke.

## The Royal Family

This toast is much less commonly proposed. Again, no speech is required, but the proposer usually gives the toast in the following form:

Ladies and gentlemen – I have the honour to propose the toast of the — and the other members of the Royal Family.

The exact wording of this toast naturally depends on royal births, marriages and deaths. However, there is no prescribed formula according to rank, and when the toast is to be given the chairperson should ascertain the current form beforehand. This is issued officially from Buckingham Palace with the approval of the Queen, changes being notified as they occur.

The toasts of the Queen and the Royal Family are the only two loyal toasts that are authorised.

# Her Majesty's Forces

This is usually proposed by the chairperson. Obviously there must be a patriotic ring about this speech, but it should not be overdone and there must be no suspicion of bombast. The proper note to strike is quiet, sober sincerity, without any striving after effect. If the proposer has served in the Forces, a little gentle humour may be introduced as relief, but it must not be either pompous or patronising. If the proposer has never served in the Forces, humour is best avoided, and gratitude and respect should be expressed.

## *Specimen*

Ladies and gentlemen – It is a truism to say that in a time of peace the Armed Forces can never be popular. They cost our Exchequer large sums of money and, seemingly, show little return on the investment. Perhaps the real return is what does not show. Britain has been at peace for half a century, no great stretch of time perhaps; nevertheless greater than any this country has known for 250 years. This peace has not just happened, but has, in large part, been earned by the professionalism, skill and steadfastness of purpose of our sailors, soldiers and airmen.

The character of war has changed, and modern war is total war. But let us not forget that the grim business of fighting is still done by the Armed Forces. And civilians, whatever their own efforts, are in the eternal debt of the men and women who have gone out to grapple with the enemy on land, at sea, and in the air.

The world around, in Malaya and Borneo, Bahrain and Oman, Kenya, the Falkland Islands, Bermuda and Belize, they have faithfully served our interests and the interests of our friends. With anarchy and the mindless use of terror ever on the increase, sadly we now need them more than ever at home in the most thankless of tasks. They have for years hazarded and given their lives in Northern Ireland to preserve the integrity of this realm. They protect our airports from scenes of bloody massacre and our vulnerable off-shore oil from terrorist attack. Theirs is a major contribution to the strength of that North Atlantic Treaty Organisation which has, since the Second World War, deterred any military venture from aggressive nations of the world.

Our forces are not numerically large but, as Goliath found out, size is not everything. Their great strength, I think, lies mainly in their efficiency and in their high morale. They have a sense of duty and a sense of purpose which is a strength to our nation. Real discipline stems from individual self-discipline, and it is this latter quality that has made our servicemen and women our finest ambassadors in every part of the world to which duty has taken them.

The toast is to Her Majesty's Forces, and I do not want to discriminate between the different services that together protect our nation and our freedom. Our debt is the same to them all and to them as a whole, not in parts. Ladies and gentleman, I give you the toast of Her Majesty's Forces and I have pleasure in coupling with it the name of our distinguished guest —.

## Useful quotations

Nothing is more binding than the friendship of companions-in-arms. – *Hillard*

The commonwealth of Venice in their armoury have this inscription: 'Happy is that city which in time of peace thinks of war.' – *Robert Burton*

Nothing except a battle lost can be half so melancholy as a battle won. – *Duke of Wellington*

There never was a good war or a bad peace. – *Benjamin Franklin*

War is nothing more than a reflection or image of the soul. It is the fiend within coming out. – *Channing*

If you want to go into battle, have an Englishman at your right hand, and another at your left, and two immediately in front and two close behind. There is something in the English which seems to guarantee security. Never forget that, even when you are most irritated by the antics of these engaging madmen. – *Voltaire*

This England never did, nor never shall,
Lie at the proud foot of a conqueror. – *William Shakespeare*

He who loves not his country can love nothing. – *Lord Byron*

Danger for danger's sake is senseless. – *J.H. Leigh Hunt*

# Reply to the Toast of Her Majesty's Forces

The reply will be made by a serving member of one of the Forces. Whatever service he or she belongs to the basic unity of the three Forces should be stressed, and tribute paid to auxiliary services.

## *Specimen*

Mr Chairman (or Madam Chair), ladies and gentlemen – The task of replying to this most generous toast fills me with both pride and alarm. Of the two, I think the alarm is stronger. In the Army we try to keep in step, but we do not all speak with one voice. Heaven forbid! But now I am called upon to speak, not only for the whole of the British Army, but for the Royal Navy and the Royal Air Force as well. The task is too heavy for me and I must ask you to allow me to speak simply for myself.

I would like to say that while I am dismayed at having to reply to this toast, I warmly support the form in which it has been proposed. You have honoured the three services as one whole and that, I think, is how they should be considered. Of course each service has its own traditions and customs and different expertise, but at heart we are pretty well at one.

I do not want to suggest that there is no such thing as inter-service rivalry. On the contrary, and it is very keen – and, I think, a good thing. Co-operation and competition are sometimes regarded as opposites, but in the services they stimulate each other. And as for service rivalry – well, believe me, the rivalry between the Army and the Navy or Air Force is quite tame compared with the rivalry between two of our crack regiments!

We in the services have a common goal, which is to serve the nation. No one is born into the Armed Forces. We come, be it for three years or thirty, from every walk of life, schoolchildren, milkmen, miners, farmers, factory workers, engineers, doctors, dentists. We come from every corner of the country and from every kind of home. From these countless diverse threads is woven a whole cloth, that takes no colour of vested or sectional interest but serves the common good.

On behalf of this fabric, known as Her Majesty's Forces, I thank you.

## The Royal Navy

Usually proposed by the chair, again the keynote here is sober patriotism. If the proposer of the toast is serving or has served in the Army or RAF, he or she can brighten up the speech with some friendly inter-service chaffing. This shouldn't be overdone, however, and the speech should end on a note of sincere respect. If the proposer is not an ex-serviceman or woman, jokes shouldn't be made at the expense of the service. Historical allusions can be brought in if you wish, but should be used sparingly.

### *Specimen*

Ladies and gentlemen – I now have the honour to propose the toast of the Silent Service, the Royal Navy. Well may it be silent for it has no need to boast aloud. Its deeds have always spoken for themselves. From the days of the Armada to the Battle of the Atlantic, it held the supremacy of the sea. In recent times, the extreme power and technical ingenuity of weapon systems has changed the face of naval strategy beyond recognition.

Today, so I am told, one missile destroyer would out-gun, out-range and out-run the most powerful capital ship of the Second World War. The modern nuclear submarine runs at depths and speeds for distances not dreamed of at the time of the Battle of the Atlantic and may carry a million times the destructive potential of a submarine of that era. With weapons such as these and others, our Navy continues to guarantee the security and freedom of these British Isles.

Though fewer in number than in years gone by, White Ensigns can still be seen from pole to pole, and in every ocean. Wherever they are seen there is a reaction: among the British, one of pride and affection; among our friends, one of welcome; with others, great circumspection. All, though, have one element in common, and that is respect.

From the days of King Alfred, the Navy has carried the responsibility for the defence of this island's long coastline and our shipping lanes. In recent years, to these demanding duties it has added both the defence of our seabed resources and assumed the role of shield-bearer to the nation with responsibility for our strategic nuclear deterrent.

In the old days we spoke of ships of oak and hearts of oak. Nowadays our ships are of steel; and it is not too much to say that the staunchness of our sailors has evolved in a like manner with their ships. Nothing but iron courage and nerves of steel can stand the strain of naval warfare today.

Our Navy is a force of which we can be more justly proud today than ever before. I ask you, ladies and gentlemen, to drink the health of the Royal Navy and I couple with the toast the name of —.

## Useful quotations

The best thing I know between France and England is the sea. – *Douglas Jerrold*

A new recruit, on putting to sea and suffering with sickness said afterwards that for the first day he was afraid he would die, and the second day he was afraid he wouldn't. – *Anon*

Thank God, I have done my duty. – *Horatio Nelson*

*See also under* Her Majesty's Forces.

## Reply to the Toast of The Royal Navy

### *Specimen*

Mr Chairman (or Madam Chair), ladies and gentlemen – I must apologise for standing up and breaking the naval tradition which has just been so warmly praised. I have been reminded that the service to which I have the honour of belonging is famous for its silence. Such a compliment deserves a more appropriate reply than a speech.

Indeed, there is nothing I wish to say beyond expressing my thanks for the generosity of the toast and the most cordial way in which you have received it. I would add only this: service in the British Navy is a great privilege as well as a responsibility. In playing our part in the defence of the country we have always known that we have the trust and confidence of the British people behind us. This means a lot to us and, come what may, I promise you that we shall try to continue to be worthy of this trust.

Ladies and gentlemen, on behalf of the Royal Navy, I thank you.

## The British Army

This toast is usually proposed by the chairperson. *See under* The Royal Navy.

### *Specimen*

Ladies and gentlemen – Khaki is not a glamorous colour and glamour is not a word that comes to mind when you think of soldiers. Of the three services, the Army is probably the least showy and spectacular, but it is certainly not the least necessary or the least deserving of our admiration. Even in the atomic age, warfare is still fundamentally territorial and the control of land lies in the hands of the soldiers.

We have reason to be proud of our Army though its exists, as it were, in spite of our natural inclination. We are not a militarily minded nation. We do not glory in regimentation. This makes it all the more remarkable how many of our best young men and women voluntarily put on the uniform and execute the duties we require of them with a maximum of efficiency and a minimum of fuss.

All around the world there are many examples, even today, of how nations without the will to defend what they believe in, succumb to hostile neighbours. In the developed democratic countries the use of terrorism to disrupt and subvert the rule of law increases almost day to day. Within our own realm it is to this problem that the Army has, above all else, been addressed in the last 10 years. Sadly, there can be no doubt that without their intervention a part of the United Kingdom would have lapsed into anarchy and chaos. We have required this effort of them and the cost of it is measured in the dead that they have left on the streets of Belfast.

Abroad the Army continues to serve British interests, and to work closely with our NATO allies. Professionalism, courage, daring, endurance and respect for the rule of law remain the hallmarks of British soldiers. These are hallmarks that are a source of pride to the rest of us and are respected wherever else in the world they may serve.

Ladies and gentlemen, I give you the toast of our Army, coupled with the name of —.

### Useful quotations

I don't know what effect these men may have on the enemy, but, by Gad, they frighten me! – *Duke of Wellington, inspecting his troops before Waterloo*

We're in the Final now. – *Unknown British soldier after the evacuation from Dunkirk in 1940*

*See also under* Her Majesty's Forces.

## Reply to the Toast of the British Army

### *Specimen*

Mr Chairman (or Madam Chair), ladies and gentlemen – I wish to thank you most sincerely for the way that you have responded to this toast. As a professional soldier I find it heartening to hear such kind words from one of my employers and I am glad to think that you have value for money. I am glad too that you have not clothed the military machine with any false glamour. We know we are, at best, a necessary evil. We produce nothing, we consume a lot, and we cost a good deal. We occupy valuable ground, we take up housing accommodation, we have to be clothed and fed, and we can offer nothing in return unless the country happens to be in danger of attack.

I assure you that no one wishes more earnestly than the professional that there were no need to retain an army. As Wellington said, 'Next to a battle lost, the saddest thing is a battle won.' However, you Mr Chairman (or Madam Chair) have remarked, the need does remain and as long as the need remains so shall we.

Before concluding I should like to say a word or two about our soldiers. Much is made today about the declining sense of values in our young people. I can only say that in the Army we see little of it. It is not only a responsibility, it is also a very real pleasure to command young men and women with the standards of dedication and professionalism that our young soldiers constantly show.

Ladies and gentlemen, on behalf of the Army, I thank you for your generous welcome to this toast.

# The Royal Air Force

This toast is usually proposed by the chairperson. *See under* The Royal Navy.

## *Specimen*

Ladies and gentlemen – Our nation is steeped in tradition and nowhere is this more apparent than in the Armed Forces. Both our Navy and Army have long and glorious histories. The history of our Air Force is much shorter but certainly not less glorious. It has shown that tradition does not depend on antiquity, for, young as it is, the RAF has already established its own distinctive tradition. This country has had to fight many critical battles in order to remain free; some of these have become epics in our history. The Navy had its Trafalgar, the Army had its Waterloo, and the RAF had the Battle of Britain. In each of these battles the enemy fought with a superior strength. In each the tenacity and will to win, which shows something of what is best in the nation, carried the day.

Since the last war there have been those who have claimed that the development of the ballistic missile has made all air forces obsolete. Time and technology have shown them to be quite wrong. The security of our skies from many forms of attack, the support of our Army and Navy in the work that they do and the flexible response that the intricacies of today's politics require can only be achieved by good aircraft flown by the best people.

Ladies and gentlemen, I give you the toast of the Royal Air Force, coupled with the name of —.

## *Useful quotations*

Never in the field of human conflict was so much owed by so many to so few. – *Winston Churchill*

*See also under* Her Majesty's Forces.

# Reply to the Toast of the Royal Air Force

## *Specimen*

Mr Chairman (or Madam Chair), ladies and gentlemen – Thank you indeed for your kind words. You have referred to us as a young service. But it is also true that, as a service, we have more experience of air operations all over the world than any other air force. It is a service of which I am proud to be a part.

When one thinks of the Royal Air Force there is a tendency to think only of the aircraft and those who fly them. Today, more than ever, the flying of an aircraft is the result of teamwork. The public see only the pilot and the aircraft, but without the effective support of the unseen group of fitters, technicians, air traffic control staff, radar engineers and ground maintenance staff, both pilot and aircraft would fail very rapidly. The work of the ground staff is hard and monotonous, and often goes unappreciated, by the public at least. But it is appreciated by the aircrew, for our lives depend on their efficiency, and we live to be grateful to them.

It is on behalf of this whole team that I thank you, ladies and gentlemen, for the welcome that you have given to this toast.

# The County Regiment

This toast is usually proposed by the chairperson. *See under Her Majesty's Forces.* The appeal will, of course, be of a local or regional nature.

## *Specimen*

Ladies and gentlemen – In these days of centralisation, the county does not mean as much as it once did. Indeed, in recent years, some of our ancient county names have disappeared, probably forever. I am not going to say whether that is a good or a bad thing, but I must say that I think it would be very bad if county divisions disappeared altogether. Fortunately we can be sure that this will never happen. The MCC would not allow it!

However, not only have some county boundaries disappeared, but many of the old county regiments have marched past for the last time before being amalgamated with another unit – or disbanded. I do not believe that this will ever happen to our regiment. With help from our friends in Whitehall and, as you know, there are no more stubborn defenders of last ditches than Whitehall Warriors, the future of our regiment remains assured. But our friends are shrewd as well as stubborn. They know the value of local patriotism.

When a recruit joins the Army he or she becomes a number, but his or her regiment has a name. Our county regiment has not only a name but also an honourable history. You know if its famous exploits of the distant, and especially of the more recent, past. I know that no one will challenge me when I say that its record will stand comparison with that of any other regiment in the Army.

In every action our regiment has acquitted itself well, with the qualities of courage and dash, grit and determination. I am not suggesting that these qualities are given at birth to everyone who is lucky enough to be born in our county, but I do say that they are traditional in the county regiment and they are the first things that every new recruit learns to appreciate. I know that you all share my hope that our regiment will not have to fight another action. It can afford to rest on its laurels and it is our hope that it will be allowed to do so. But if it ever has to be tested again – well, we all know it will again make the name of our county resound all over the land.

Ladies and gentlemen, I give you the toast of the — Regiment and I couple with it the name of Colonel —.

## *Useful quotations*

It is true we are creatures of circumstance, but circumstances are also, in a great measure, the creatures of us. – *Lord Lytton*

*See also under* Her Majesty's Forces and The British Army.

# Reply to the toast of the County Regiment

## *Specimen*

Mr Chairman (or Madam Chair), ladies and gentlemen – I am proud to be able to reply to a toast to the regiment that I have the honour to command. It is a great honour, and I am always conscious of it.

Within our regiment, as many here will know, we find a continuity of service across the generations. We also find in many cases within this generation other ties of kinship. In fair part because of this, it is my firm belief that we have the finest officers, the finest NCOs and the finest soldiers in the whole British Army. With such a composition, a regiment can triumph over everything. We have just been told that the county is proud of the regiment and I must assure you that the regiment is very proud of the county. Not only does it give us our name, it also binds us together. It means that if we are called upon to fight to defend Britain we shall be fighting together to defend the same part which we all hold so dear.

On behalf of —, thank you.

# The Royal Naval Volunteer Reserve

This toast is usually proposed by the chairperson. *See under* The Royal Navy and The Territorials.

## *Specimen*

Ladies and gentlemen – It is my privilege tonight to propose the toast to the Royal Naval Volunteer Reserve. This is not a very common toast because the RNVR is usually included in the more general toast to the Royal Navy. I know that members of the Reserve are happy to be thought of as part of the Navy; equally the Navy is proud to include their company.

Whatever praise our Navy deserves and it can hardly be praised too highly, is due equally to the Volunteer Reserve. These two words tell the whole story. On the one hand it is a voluntary service and its members give their time and effort to help in the vital work of safeguarding our country. On the other hand it is a reserve. That means it is liable to be called to full-time duty only when such duty is likely to be most arduous and dangerous. It follows from these definitions that every member of the RNVR is a person of high patriotism in the finest sense of the word, capable of genuine self-sacrifice and of real courage. Those who do not possess these qualities would never join the Reserve.

I do not need to remind you of the work of the RNVR in two world wars. The deeds of the service are enshrined in the history of the Royal Navy. Today they stand ready to serve again on our behalf, particularly in the dangerous task of sweeping mines from our coastal waters. If these gallant volunteers are called upon we know that they will serve with the same spirit as they have done in the past.

Ladies and gentlemen, I give you the toast of the Royal Naval Volunteer Reserve coupled with the name of —.

### *Useful quotations*
*See under* The Royal Navy and Her Majesty's Forces.

# Reply to the Toast of the Royal Naval Volunteer Reserve

### *Specimen*
Mr Chairman (or Madam Chair), ladies and gentlemen – the Royal Navy is called the Silent Service, and I should hate to think of this high tradition of the professionals being disgraced by an amateur like me. All I can say in reply to your generous toast is that we are proud to belong, in a small way, to the Navy. We do not deserve the particular compliments you have paid us, for service in the Reserve involves no real hardship and offers great satisfaction. It is, as you say, a voluntary service, which means that we are in it because we want to be and because we like it.

On behalf of the RNVR I thank you for the cordial welcome you have given to this toast.

# The Territorial Army

This toast is usually proposed by the chairperson. At a function given specially for a unit of the Territorial Army this toast is, of course, of great importance. It may also be proposed at a more general civic function or at a purely social function attended by a number of Territorials. The toast should then be proposed in a lighter and less formal way, but whatever the occasion the speaker should bring in the local as well as the national aspect of the Territorial Army. *See also under* The Royal Navy.

## *Specimen*

Ladies and gentlemen – I do not think any regular soldier is likely to quarrel with me when I say that the nation could not get on without the Territorial Army. I hesitate to say that without the Territorials we could not survive, because the phrase is greatly overworked and in this century we have several times been in circumstances in which survival was theoretically impossible. But I can say with certainty that our survival and our continued freedom and prosperity owe a great deal to this volunteer army of ours.

Patriotism is a word that has been often abused, and the term 'a great patriot' is sometimes applied to those whose love of their country has been professed only in words. It should be reserved for those who are prepared to make personal sacrifices; and I do not think it is any exaggeration to say that every man or woman who joins the Territorials is a great patriot. Territorials volunteer for a service that brings them only modest financial rewards, that may cause them considerable inconvenience; and that certainly makes substantial demands on their leisure time. They do this in the full knowledge that in the event of war, they will be called upon to stand up to the first onslaught by the aggressor, while a citizen army is created and trained behind the lines.

In two world wars our Territorial Army has had to carry out this task, and each time it has done it with valour and efficiency. We all hope that it will be spared a further sacrifice of this sort; and it is our best guarantee against such a tragedy that our Territorial Army should be strong, well trained, and well equipped. The need for the Territorials has in no way decreased, despite the restrictions under which it now operates.

We have national pride in our Territorial Army, and civic pride in our own — (local Territorial unit). We owe it to these fine people to express our pride in the form of practical gratitude.

Ladies and gentlemen, I ask you to drink to the health of the Territorial Army, coupling with it the names of — and —.

### Useful quotations

*See under* Her Majesty's Forces and The British Army.

# Reply to the Toast of The Territorial Army

### Specimen

Mr Chairman (or Madam Chair), ladies and gentlemen – I feel greatly honoured to reply to this toast which has been proposed in such generous terms, but I hope that you will not think I am being discourteous when I venture to contradict one statement that has been made about us. You have said that our service brings no reward. We think it does. We in the TA enjoy sport and outdoor activities; we enjoy being under canvas; and above all, we enjoy comradeship and the knowledge that we are doing something useful. Nor are we out of pocket on the deal. Certainly the sums of money that we receive for our services are small, but to this must be added the benefits of travel to many interesting places.

More seriously, we are conscious that the responsibilities of the TA are now greater than at any time since the Second World War. This certainly makes the job all the more rewarding and satisfying to us. We thoroughly enjoy our life in the Territorials, and if there are those of you out there who want to find a way of using your spare time without having to pay for the pleasure I strongly recommend you to join us. The work is most worthwhile and the comradeship is in excess of anything that most of us find in our life outside.

On behalf of the Territorial Army and of the — (unit) in particular I thank you for the way in which you have received this toast.

## Our Noble Selves

This is a toast to a particular regiment, battery or squadron. It is used at a reunion where no outsiders are present, and is generally proposed by the chairperson. While the speech must have a ring of sincerity, it can be pleasantly informal and the speaker should try to evoke happy memories of comradeship.

### *Specimen*

Ladies and gentlemen – It is my great privilege to propose the toast of the finest unit in the British Army. Of course I do not need to say which unit I am speaking of. I know it was the finest unit when I served in it. I believe it was the finest unit before I served in it. And I am sure that many of my old comrades will be quick to tell me that it cannot help but be even finer now that I am out of it!

Old soldiers, I know, are expected to fade away. I am happy to say that I see no sign of any fading here tonight. On the contrary, unless my memory fails me, it seems to me that most of the old soldiers whom I knew when they were younger are now looming larger than ever.

Not all of us here tonight served in the — at the same time. Not all of us have the same memories. No doubt some of the most stirring deeds that took place in my time have failed to be passed down to the next generation. It is even possible that the present members of the unit have never heard of (here insert a reference to a humorous incidence connected with someone present at the function), or of (insert another similar reference). If these things have been forgotten, then I feel I am at least serving some purpose in recalling them.

Ladies and gentlemen, I am not going to bang a drum in praise of the —. It does not need it. We have never advertised our glories to outsiders, and we do not have to advertise them to ourselves. We have a great history, and I am sure that we have a great future. Before I close I must ask you to think of our proudest but saddest possession: our roll of honour. It includes names that are familiar to most of us – names of those whom we should like to have here tonight. Let us pay homage to them, above all, as we drink – to the —!

### Useful quotations

Be sure to leave other men their turns to speak. – *Francis Bacon*

*See under* Her Majesty's Forces and The British Army.

# The Women's Services

This is a general toast, like the toast to Her Majesty's Forces. Toasts to the particular branches of the Women's Services are given on the following pages. All these toasts are invariably given by men, usually by members of the Forces. The keynote of each speech should be appreciation of the work women do, and the speaker must be careful to avoid any hint of patronage or condescension.

### Specimen

Ladies and gentlemen – Serving one's country, like voting, used to be a man's job alone. The women's job was to keep the home fires burning; and if it had been left to the men, that is all they would still be doing. For no one can say that the men dragged them out of their homes, any more than it could be said that women were dragged to the polls. The Women's Services came into being as a result of the demand of the women themselves. That demand was conceded rather grudgingly, and with many shakings of heads, by men who were convinced in advance that women would never make soldiers.

I do not need to remind you of the way in which the Women's Services have proved themselves. They served with great distinction in two world wars. They have since gone on from strength to strength. Today they find themselves increasingly being integrated into almost every job that the men do.

Many servicemen are inclined at first to think of their probable value as mainly ornamental, but the truth is they are in uniform to do a job of work, and the way they do their job wins the admiration of us all. After the First World War the Women's Services were stood down. They returned for the Second World War and made themselves so indispensable that they gained their permanent peacetime establishments. They have won their colours the hard way, and now the men of the Forces are proud to acknowledge them as their comrades in uniform.

Ladies and gentlemen, I ask you to join me in this salute to the gallant women – I should prefer to call them ladies, but they would not allow it – of the Services!

### Useful quotations

The female woman is one of the greatest institutions of which this land can boast. – *Artemus Ward*

Great women belong to history and to self-sacrifice. – *J.H. Hunt*

Nature was in earnest when she made women. – *O.W. Holmes*

*See also under* Her Majesty's Forces and The Ladies.

## Reply to the Toast of the Women's Services

### Specimen

Mr Chairman (or Madam Chair), ladies and gentlemen – Thank you for the kind way in which you have received this toast. I would almost suspect you of flattery – and being a woman, I should not seriously object to that – were it not for the fact that in my service life I have had so many proofs of the goodwill of the men's services. It is true, I agree, that we had to demand to be allowed to share in the defence of our country, and in the early days we faced much opposition from some people who thought we weren't up to the job, and perhaps shouldn't even want the job. Today we are for the most part accepted by our male colleagues and work happily alongside them.

I must say how much we appreciate the way in which the men take us seriously, trust us to do our jobs, and leave us to get on with them. Our contribution is different from that of the men who go out and fight, but we are proud to play our part in the protection of our land.

On behalf of the Women's Services, I thank you.

## The Women's Royal Army Corps

This toast is usually proposed by a member of the Army. *See under* The Women's Services.

### *Specimen*

Ladies and gentlemen – Before I ask you to join me in this very important toast, I want to tell you a very short – and true – story about two young soldiers. One of them was a handsome, dashing young fellow who greatly fancied himself as a lady-killer. The other was a more serious lad, who had no girlfriends, and described himself as a confirmed bachelor and even a woman-hater.

These two soldiers were serving in the same unit, and one day they heard the news that they were to be reinforced by members of the Women's Royal Army Corps. The lady-killer was delighted. 'Just what we need,' he said with an anticipatory gleam in his eyes. The woman-hater threw up his hands in despair. 'At least I thought I should be safe from that in the Army,' he complained grumpily.

A month later the two soldiers exchanged opinions again. The lady-killer looked more subdued, and even a little crestfallen. 'These girls are useless – they don't know what they're here for,' he grumbled. His comrade, who had lost his despair, answered thoughtfully, 'Oddly enough, that's just what they do know.'

The moral, I think, is clear enough; but just to make it clear that the girls are more human than our lady-killer thought, I had better add that within three months of their arrival, the woman-hater married one of them!

You all know what these girls did during the war. In those days, when many of them shared soldiers' dangers in mixed batteries, they were called Auxiliaries. They proved themselves much more than that, and they have deservedly become an Army Corps in their own right.

Ladies and gentlemen, I ask you to drink to the health of the Women's Royal Army Corps, and with this toast I couple the name of —.

### Useful quotations

*See under* The Women's Services and The Ladies.

## Reply to the Toast of the Women's Royal Army Corps

### Specimen

Ladies and gentlemen – Thank you for your kindness. You have, I think, honoured us too highly. We are proud of our service and honoured to be an independent corps in the British Army. We try to be good soldiers and to work to the best of our abilities alongside the men.

Fortunately we do not have to compete, because the men are so co-operative. While we might operate in different spheres as operations demand, most of us serve in mixed units where we work hand in hand with men. Not that we need our hands holding, but you know what I mean!

On behalf of the Corps, thank you.

## The Women's Royal Naval Service

This toast is usually proposed by a member of the Royal Navy. See under The Women's Services. The story in the specimen toast of the Women's Royal Army Corps can be adapted by changing the reference to two soldiers to two sailors.

## Specimen

Ladies and gentlemen – Britannia, whom we tell to rule the waves, is a lady; and a very warlike lady, too. Our picture of a Wren is less fierce – although this may be deceptive – and a good deal more charming. But then the Wrens do not try to rule the waves. They simply keep in order the men who sail over them.

The Navy has the honour of being the Senior Service and the reputation of being the most hidebound in tradition. This reputation is a bit exaggerated. According to some popular views, you might think that most sailors are still bewailing the days of the windjammers and complaining about newfangled idea of steam. But it is true that the Navy has its roots deep in the past, and traditions of the service die hard. Yet no tradition died so quickly as the idea that the place of women was in the home – or rather in the next port. The Wrens came; we saw them; and they conquered.

Please do not mistake me about the nature of their conquest. It was not merely a case of sailors falling for a pretty face after staring at each other's ugly mugs – and not that the Wrens' faces aren't pretty. But I don't need to tell you that here! The real reason why the Wrens won our salt-stained hearts is that they do a job of work in what I can only call a sailor-like fashion. It is not just that they are efficient – although they certainly are. It's not just that they work hard and take their service seriously, although they do. It's that in a way that is almost uncanny, they have grasped the very spirit of the Navy right from the beginning, and become part of it almost as if they had always belonged. It is this that makes it so easy for us to accept and appreciate them; and now it is hard indeed to think of the Navy without them.

Ladies and gentlemen – to the Wrens, God bless 'em!

## Useful quotations

*See under* The Women's Services and The Ladies.

## Reply to the Toast of the
## Women's Royal Naval Service

### *Specimen*

Ladies and gentlemen – Pride, I know, is a dangerous thing, but I must tell you frankly that I have never got over my pride in belonging to the Wrens. I don't think any of us has. Britain is a seafaring nation, and the glories of our Navy reach the hearts of British women as well as British men.

Please don't think that we imagine ourselves the successors of the great sailor-heroes of our history. We know that our own part in the service of the Navy is small if important. But the fact that we have a part at all is to us a great privilege and honour. Most important of all is the recognition that we get from the Navy itself. I only hope we shall always be worthy of the service.

On behalf the Wrens, ladies and gentlemen, I thank you most sincerely.

## The Women's Royal Air Force

This toast is usually proposed by a member of the Royal Air Force. See under The Women's Services. The story in the specimen toast of the Women's Royal Army Corps can be easily adapted by changing the reference to two soldiers to two airmen.

### *Specimen*

Ladies and gentlemen – Nothing gives me greater pleasure than to propose the health of the Women's Royal Air Force. I should like to give you a little talk entitled 'WRAFs whom I have met ' – and believe me, I have met some stunning types; but I understand that this would not be quite in accordance with my present duties. The Women's Royal Air Force, as various of its members have told me several times, does not exist for the solace and entertainment of the RAF. Its purpose is to do a job of work.

Now let me stop fooling and tell you that we really do appreciate the work these women do. Please don't get the idea they are just glorified air hostesses. They are highly trained and highly skilled technicians, and when we go up in the air our safety depends on them. You may rest assured that we have full confidence in their ability and their sense of responsibility. They do not let us down – they keep us up!

Ladies and gentlemen, I ask you to drink to the health of the Women's Royal Air Force, and I couple with this toast the name of —.

### Useful quotations

*See under* The Women's Services and The Ladies.

## Reply to the Toast of the Women's Royal Air Force

### Specimen

Ladies and gentlemen – Thank you very much for the reception you have given to this toast. As you know, we used to be called Auxiliaries; and it was only after the Second World War that we were made into a service in our own right. I hope you will not think that this has made us get above ourselves. Whatever our name, we know that our function now is the same as it was during the days when the RAF was fighting the Battle of Britain – to help protect our country from the air.

The whole nation is rightly proud of the achievements of the RAF. Everyone knows our debt to the service. I hope you will not blame us if we bask a little in reflected glory. We do not overrate our contribution to the total effort, but we do have the privilege of service with the RAF in all facets of its operations. If we do just a little to help them – and we like to think we do – then we are immensely proud of it.

The proposer of this toast has said some kind things about us, and not only from the strictly service point of view. He has reminded you that we are women, but that the RAF does take us seriously, and this makes our work worthwhile. We shall go on doing our best.

On behalf of the Women's Royal Air Force, thank you very much.

# The Nursing Services

Simple admiration is the keynote of this speech, and the praise should be sincere rather than extravagant.

## *Specimen*

Ladies and gentlemen – I have great pleasure in proposing the toast of the Nursing Services. This toast hardly needs a speech, for our debt to the Nursing Services is too well known. Nursing the sick is service in its highest form – service involving hard work and bringing little material reward. It demands unselfishness, a will to work, and above all a sense of vocation.

Our nurses are our champions in peace and war. They receive few decorations. All too often they are taken for granted. While we rightly revere the name of Florence Nightingale, we are all too apt to overlook the fact that the tradition of the 'Lady of the Lamp' is still carried on. And of course we have men *and* women in this branch of the services whose courage and devotion are integral parts of the very spirit of the Nursing Services today.

Our nurses prefer to carry out their tasks anonymously, and they seek no praise. I shall not embarrass them further. Ladies and gentlemen, I ask you to drink to the health of the Nursing Services, and I couple with this toast the name of Sister —.

## *Useful quotations*

*See under* The Women's Services and The Ladies.

# Reply to the Toast of the Nursing Services

## *Specimen*

Ladies and gentlemen – Thank you for the kind welcome you have given to this toast. Really I think it was too kind, for we nurses are very ordinary beings. I am not going to pretend that nursing is not hard work, or that we don't sometimes find it tedious; but by and large we do it because we like it, and that seems a good reason for doing any job. For anyone who didn't like the work I imagine it would be pretty hateful, but for our part we count ourselves to be doing something that appeals to us.

And I must add a word about our patients. I expect that most of you will have been in our hands at some time or other, so I can make it quite personal when I say that for the most part we like our patients. There are a few exceptions, of course – and in my experience the biggest grumblers are the ones who have the least wrong with them. Many of the most seriously ill cases that I have nursed have shown such appreciation and good humour that it was a positive joy to do what little I could to ease their suffering. For although a doctor, and especially a surgeon, may have to consider the disease more than the patient, for we nurses sickness is a very human matter; and I know of no finer sight in the world than a sick person smiling bravely in spite of suffering. It is that sort of sight that makes nursing really worthwhile.

On behalf of the Nursing Services, ladies and gentlemen, thank you.

# CHAPTER SIX

# Civic Toasts

## The Mayor and Corporation

This toast is generally proposed at a civic dinner or other function, where the Mayor will be known personally by many of those present. A personal element should therefore be introduced into the speech. For example, if it is known that the Mayor is a keen golfer some humorous reference could be made to the fact.

### *Specimen*

Mr Chairman (or Madam Chair), ladies and gentlemen. I am happy to have the duty of proposing the toast of the Mayor and Corporation. Most of us, I am afraid, are in the habit of taking the Corporation for granted. What is worse, on the few occasions when we do think about it, our thoughts are not always kindly. We remember the Corporation when there are elections – and then, of course, the Corporation remembers us. And we remember it especially when we get the demands for our Council Tax. Otherwise we seem to forget that the Corporation exists. My only defence for this apparently ungrateful attitude is that it shows, far better than any words could do, just how efficiently the Corporation does its work. It never lets us down.

But although we may take the Corporation for granted, the same does not apply to the Mayor. He is not the sort of man you can ignore. He is a personality, a character. He leaves his mark on everything he does. If you do not believe me, go up to the golf course and have a look at the bunker behind the green at the fifteenth hole. There you will see what worshipful niblick did three months ago.

But I am not being fair. Our Mayor, as you know, is tireless in the performance of his many public duties, and we have every reason to be grateful to him. Both he and all the members of the Corporation labour unstintingly for the good of the community. They set a magnificent example in local government – and I only wish that the governments of the world were in similar hands.

Ladies and gentlemen, I ask you to drink to the health of our Major and Corporation.

## Reply to the Toast of the Mayor and Corporation

### *Specimen*

Mr Chairman (or Madam Chair), ladies and gentlemen. You are very kind, much kinder than we deserve. We of the Corporation are not particularly modest folk, but I am sure my colleagues will want me to say that we have not earned all your compliments. The fact is that we do comparatively little. The real work is done by the various officers who put local government into effect. I know that the standard of local government in this country is exceptionally high, but I am convinced that it is nowhere higher than it is here.

But I fear I am doing an injustice to my colleagues. They do work – really hard, not only on their own account, but also by helping and supporting me. When I first took office I was, frankly, quite nervous about the workload I was assuming. But I needn't have worried. Certainly there are numerous duties to perform, but thanks to the guidance and support of the team around me I have been able to tackle them all with enthusiasm, and, I hope I may say, a modicum of success.

Therefore, ladies and gentlemen, it is with some pangs of conscience on my own behalf – but not on behalf of my colleagues – that I thank you most sincerely for the cordial reception you have given to this toast.

# Her Majesty's Judges

The task of proposing this toast is usually given to an experienced speaker. The speech needs to be good, with some real wit, because the reply will almost certainly be an example of good oratory. Humour is essential here.

## *Specimen*

Ladies and gentlemen – The task of proposing this toast fills me with alarm. This is not because I am frightened of Her Majesty's Judges in general – certainly not through any particular fear of Mr Justice —, whom we are so happy to see here tonight. For by a fortunate chance Mr Justice — is one of Her Majesty's Judges who has never had to pass judgement on me. I do not fear him for his power, yet I may be sure you will hear a speech of great wit and eloquence which will make my present effort seem even feebler than it is.

There is a common belief in this country that judges are rather dry, inhuman people who live apart in a world of torts and malfeasances, and really have little idea of everyday life as the rest of us know it. Many judges, of course, deliberately foster this idea. For hours they sit in silence, apparently unmoved by either the eloquence of the barristers or the pathos and drama of the evidence of witnesses. You wonder if they are really alive. Then when you have almost given up hope, the Judge leans forward and, with a slightly puzzled frown, ask some such question as, 'Who is Charles Chaplin?'

This almost unbelievable ignorance – and I am stretching a point when I say that it is only almost unbelievable – contrasts strangely with the omniscience of the barristers. They know everything about everything. One day a barrister is speaking with all the authority of an economist; the next day he is arguing equally impressively on the proper way to prune roses.

Now as judges would have us believe that they know nothing about economics or pruning roses, one may wonder what they were doing before they were elevated to their high office. Where did they come from? The answer, as you know, is that they came from the Bar. Please do not misunderstand me. The Bar I am speaking of is a very dry one – dry as dust, in fact – with so much dust that the barristers even find enough to try to throw into the eyes of the jury. So that a judge who now professes ignorance even of the existence of Charles Chaplin was himself once an expert on economics, horticulture, and every other subject that comes the way of a barrister.

The explanation for this change is not so difficult to find. A barrister and a judge have only one thing in common: knowledge of the law. In at least one vitally important respect they are utterly different. The barrister prosecutes or pleads. He is frankly partisan. The judge is impartial. That, I think, is why a judge becomes a different person from the man who used to be a barrister.

Be that as it may, I am sure you will all agree with me when I say that Her Majesty's Judges enjoy not only our respect and admiration, but also our confidence.

Ladies and gentleman, I have great pleasure in asking you to drink the health of Her Majesty's Judges, and I couple with this toast the name of Mr Justice —.

## *Useful quotations*

I would be loath to cast away my speech, for beside that it is excellently penn'd I have taken great pains to con it. – *William Shakespeare*

For pity is the virtue of the law,
And none but tyrants use it cruelly. – *William Shakespeare*

The law hath not been dead, though it hath slept. – *William Shakespeare*

# The Magistrates

This speech does not call for the same standard of oratory as the toast of Her Majesty's Judges, and a more personal element may be introduced if the magistrates present are well known to the speaker and the audience.

## *Specimen*

Ladies and gentlemen – I have a vague recollection from my schooldays that when I had finished learning the dozen different ways of expressing the Latin for a table, I was put on to declining a noun called magister. I believe that it is from this word that magistrate comes; and I know that it means master.

This seems very appropriate, for in the presence of a magistrate I feel very much like a schoolboy in the presence of his master. Indeed, if I remember rightly we used to refer to our head as The Beak.

By quite extraordinary and sustained good fortune, I have not yet been brought before our magistrates. I expect this will surprise you; it is a constant source of amazement to me. But when my day does come – as I fear it must – I invite you all to come to court and hear what the clerk says when he is asked if I am known.

Perhaps because of my lack of knowledge of the magistrates in their official capacity, I am very happy to propose their health. The Bench is held in deservedly high esteem, and I am sure you will agree with me when I say that we are particularly lucky in this respect. Ladies and gentlemen, the magistrates.

## *Useful quotations*

No fools are so troublesome as those who have some wit. – *Duc de La Rochefoucauld*

It is a sad thing when men have neither wit to speak well nor judgment to hold their tongues. – *Jean de La Bruyère*

*See also under* Her Majesty's Judges.

# Reply to the Toast of the Magistrates

## *Specimen*

Ladies and gentlemen – it is a novel and refreshing experience for one to receive such cordial good wishes for my health in public. More commonly I hear expressions of hope for my early demise. From the cordial reception you have given to this toast I can only conclude that you all have very clear consciences, and that none of you expects to appear before the Bench. May I offer you my congratulations and, in return, express my hope that you will all continue to keep clear of the law.

If, however, you contemplate a life of crime, it would seem that now is an excellent time to start. You are well aware, I am sure, that magistrates are crusty folk and that the severity of the sentences they impose depends mainly on their physical well-being and the state of their livers. My criminal friends assure me that it is always better after lunch, provided that the lunch was a good one. All magistrates are bad, of course; but a well-fed magistrate is not so bad as a hungry one. A liverish magistrate is the worst of all.

At the moment I am extremely well fed, and I certainly shouldn't have the heart to send any of my fellow-diners to the galleys. But I must give you a warning. If you decide to park your car on the wrong side of the road or commit some other equally heinous offence, I urge you to do it as quickly as possible and, if you are caught – as you will be, of course – to insist on an immediate appearance in Court. If you wait until tomorrow morning you will certainly find me suffering from indigestion and very unwell indeed.

So far I have been speaking only on my own behalf. But your toast was to the Bench as a whole, and on behalf of my fellow magistrates I must speak more cautiously. I know that they would want me to express my appreciation of your hearty good wishes, because I know that they share my view that those who are privileged to assist in the administration of the law should try to earn the goodwill of the community that the law is designed to protect. British justice is something that we can all be proud of, and one of the reasons for our pride is that the magistrates have strictly limited powers. In some countries a magistrate is regarded with fear by the innocent as well as the guilty; here, I think I can say, even the guilty have no need to fear that they will get any worse punishment than they deserve.

Ladies and gentlemen, thank you again.

## The Police Force

This toast is usually proposed at a function of local interest, such as a municipal dinner. In such circumstances the speaker is usually a member of the municipal council who is not connected with the police. The subject offers plenty of scope for humour, but this should not be overdone. It is important that a genuine tribute to the work of the police force should be included.

### *Specimen*

Ladies and gentlemen – When American visitors come to this country and are asked for their impressions, many of them – especially the women – begin by saying, 'I think your police are wonderful.' For some peculiar reason this is generally regarded as a huge joke. Why it should be I cannot imagine, for I am not an American visitor, or even a women, and I have never ceased to think that our police are wonderful.

Of course I must admit that I am prejudiced. Although I have lived a long life of crime, I have never been found out. Please don't think that this is because the police aren't up to their job. I am just the exception that proves the rule and I hope that if I go on saying nice things about them, the police will allow me to remain exceptional.

So far I have had only one brush with the police, and that was not really a brush. It was over a little matter of parking on the wrong day or the wrong side, or probably both. I got off with a fatherly lecture and a promise to be a good boy in future.

It is perhaps stretching a point to say that today's police are paternal, but it is nevertheless true that they always find the time to help the public, from the youngest child to the more senior members of our community. You need plenty of good humour to cope with the demands of policing, and it is rare to see a bad-tempered police officer, or one who is deliberately obstructive or officious. Watch the way the police handle a demonstration or a noisy crowd. They maintain order not by threats or blows, but by good humour and common sense. That is their peculiar genius.

Yet sometimes I wonder if we really appreciate what the Police Force does for us. I do not mean merely in its positive actions, but in its power to prevent crime. There are many views held these days on the value of punishment as a deterrent, and it is not my place to give a personal opinion on this subject. But I must express my absolute conviction that the greatest deterrent to crime is a strong and efficient Police Force. The criminal's concern about the potential punishment if caught is a secondary consideration. The thing that worries criminals most, and what makes them think twice before committing a crime, is what the chances are of their being caught. Our greatest safeguard against crime is not the severity of the law, but the figure of the police officer on the corner. And let us never forget that the police are always there, for whatever the provocation they never go on strike.

Ladies and gentlemen, I ask you to drink to the health of Police Force, and I couple with this toast the name of Inspector —.

## *Useful quotations*

When constabulary duty's to be done, a policeman's lot is not a happy one. – *Sir W.S. Gilbert*

# Reply to the Toast of the Police Force

## Specimen

Ladies and gentlemen – I am happy to reply on behalf of the Police Force to the generous welcome you have given to this toast. Flattering things have been said about us, and I am almost tempted to say that I wouldn't have the heart to arrest the proposer of the toast even if I did catch him out. But you know that policemen are said to have no hearts.

I am not going to indulge in false modesty and contradict the compliments that have been paid to the Police Force, because I am proud enough to think that it compares pretty well with the police in other countries. But the credit for this is not ours. It is yours. Nowhere in the world is there such a peaceful, law-abiding people as in Britain. A police force may be described as the discipline of the law, and discipline has to be enforced only when self-discipline is absent. You have spoken of the good-humoured way in which the police deal with noisy crowds and demonstrations. The simple fact is that humour is a wonderful tool for diffusing all but the most difficult of situations, and by and large the British public responds well to this approach.

Finally, I should like to say that we regard ourselves not only as the custodians of the peace, but also as the servants of the public. And it is a good public, and a good service to be in. Thank you, ladies and gentlemen.

# The Fire Service

*See under* The Police Force. However, there should be rather less humour, and more stress laid on the heroic nature of the fire-fighters' duties.

## Specimen

Ladies and gentlemen – I am going to let you into a secret. When I was younger and wiser – and on both counts that means many years ago – I had one great ambition in life. That was that when I grew up I should be a fire-fighter.

Well, I never achieved that ambition. That was my loss – and, no doubt, the Fire Service's gain. But I never really succeeded in conquering the desire, and today, as in those early years, I am always thrilled and excited when I see a gleaming fire engine racing along the street with its siren blaring and the fire-fighters tense and ready for action.

Fortunately I have never had to entertain the Fire Service at home in its official capacity. But I have seen it at work elsewhere, and have marvelled at the skill and courage of the men and women. And I have been over the scene of a fire after it has been put out, and I have marvelled again at the way in which property has been saved from damage. The Service's greatest work is the saving of life, and you know what heroism is shown for this purpose. But the Service also saves property, and the men and women who fight the fires show such wonderful skill and restraint – often at great personal danger – that much is preserved that would surely be lost under less careful hands.

We are lucky in this district. We have a Fire Service that can hardly have an equal in efficiency of organisation and personal zeal. It is the best insurance policy we have, because it gives us a feeling of security that could not otherwise be obtained.

Ladies and gentlemen, I ask you to drink to the men and women of our Fire Service.

## *Useful quotations*

Fire – the most tangible of all visible mysteries. – *J.H. Leigh Hunt*

Fire that's closest kept burns most of all. – *William Shakespeare*

Forewarned, forearmed; to be prepared is half the victory. – *Miguel Cervantes*

Keep the home fires burning. – *Ivor Novello*

# Reply to the Toast of the Fire Service

## *Specimen*

Ladies and gentlemen – I am happy to reply to your kind toast to the Fire Service.

I am sure I can say on behalf of everyone here connected with the service, that we feel immensely proud that we stand so high in your estimation; and immensely humble that - cliché though it may be - we achieve that simply by doing our job.

There are times when that job involves danger and risk. But equally there are times when we are called upon to observe the remains of fires that were extinguished before our arrival or had not got the strength to keep burning for us; and others when our job was to rescue a cat from an uncomfortable position which had nothing to do with fire.

But whatever the task we are called upon to undertake, I hope we will continue to earn your respect, and we acknowledge with gratitude your good wishes and admiration.

Ladies and gentlemen, on behalf of the Fire Service, I thank you.

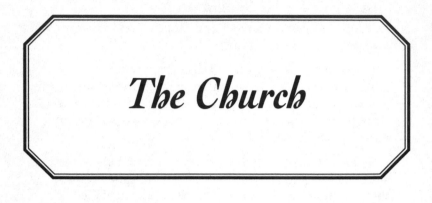

# CHAPTER SEVEN

# The Church

## The Bishop

This toast is usually proposed by the chairperson (a lay person) at a mixed gathering of clergy and laity. The theme should be the hard work put in by the clergy in general and the Bishop in particular. Humour, unless very gentle, is not recommended for any but a practised speaker, and care should be taken to avoid any controversial subject.

### Specimen

Ladies and gentlemen – It is my honour and privilege to ask you to drink to the health of our Bishop. It would be impertinent of me to try to tell you of the great work he does in our diocese, and in any case this would be impossible. You all know much of what the Bishop has done for us, but you know, too, that he does very much more which is concealed from public notice. Our Bishop does good with such stealth that he is rarely found out, even by accident. I have caught him out once or twice, but I am not going to give him away.

Tomorrow we shall have the pleasure of hearing the Bishop preach. Those who have heard him before know that this will indeed be a pleasure. But it is not merely as a great preacher that our Bishop commands our respect; it is, rather, by the example he sets us. He does not only tell us how we can lead the Christian life; by his own life he also shows us what a Christian is.

Ladies and gentlemen, I have great pleasure in proposing the health of our Bishop.

## Useful quotations

An honest man's the noblest work of God. – *Alexander Pope*

God often visits us, but most of the while we are not at home. – *Roux*

To yield reverence to another, to hold ourselves and our lives at his disposal, is the noblest state in which a man can live in this word. – *John Ruskin*

It is well said, in every sense, that a man's religion is the chief fact with regard to him. – *Thomas Carlyle*

In religion, as in friendship, they who profess most are the least sincere. – *R.B. Sheridan*

Religion is civilisation, the highest. – *Benjamin Disraeli*

Whatever makes men good Christians makes them good citizens. – *John Webster*

He whose goodness is part of himself is what is called a real man. – *Mencius*

I would rather have the affectionate regard of my fellow men than I would have heaps and mines of gold. – *Charles Dickens*

# The Clergy

*See under* The Bishop.

## Specimen

Ladies and gentlemen – It is my happy privilege to propose the health of our Bishop and clergy. Our debt to them is considerable. Not only are they are spiritual advisers and helpers, but they are also our friends. It is impossible to estimate how much good they have caused, and how much evil they have prevented, by their social work in our diocese. They would not like to hear any estimate of this kind, even if it could be made; for individually and collectively, they prefer to hide their lights under bushels.

We are very happy to have the Bishop with us today. We do not see him very often, but we know that the diocese is large and others need his presence more than we. But I must express our appreciation of the magnificent work he has done, which is the inspiration of all who try to lead a Christian life.

Ladies and gentlemen, I give the toast of the Bishop and his clergy.

# The Vicar

*See under* The Bishop. Here, however, the speech should be less formal and more humorous, as the Vicar will probably be a friend of the speaker.

## *Specimen*

Ladies and gentlemen – Popularity, like happiness, is elusive for those who seek it, and yet comes easily to those who never think about it. That is why our Vicar is such a popular man. I have never known him do or say a single thing for the sake of public favour. I have known him do and say several things that seemed likely to incur public disfavour. Yet the fact is that there is no one in this parish who is so well loved and respected as our Vicar. He is our guide, counsellor and friend – a good companion on sunny days, and a sympathetic and wise adviser and helper when things go wrong.

Our vicar is certainly not a worldly man, but he is a man of the world. I can think of no department in our parish life in which he does not play an active part. He is a star turn at our concerts. On the cricket field his leg-spinners have gained a reputation that I can only describe as unholy. His presence gives zest to every social function we have. I am told that no Women's Institute function would be worth holding without the Vicar, and I know that the ladies regard him as – well, gentlemen, there are too many husbands here for me to continue with that particular theme.

Nothing that I can say can do full justice of the Vicar, so I shall say no more, and just ask you to join me in drinking to his health. Ladies and gentlemen – the Vicar!

### Useful quotations

Blessed is the man who, having nothing to say, abstains from giving us wordy evidence of the fact. – *George Eliot*

*See also under* The Bishop.

# The Churchwardens

This toast is usually proposed by one of the clergy. Its purpose is to give recognition to the work of the laity.

### Specimen

Ladies and gentlemen – the work of the church, like the game of cricket, is shared between amateurs and professionals, or as they used to say Gentlemen and Players. Speaking as one of the least distinguished of the Players, I have the happy task of proposing the health of the Gentlemen, and in particular of those fine all-rounders the churchwardens.

My dictionary gives three definitions of a warden. The first is watchman or sentinel, the second is guardian, president, or governor, as of a college. Finally my dictionary tells me, rather surprisingly, that a warden is a kind of cooking pear.

Now, the second definition is clearly inappropriate. Our churchwardens are not presidents or governors, although I have not the slightest doubt that they would make very good ones. Nor, I think, can they be fairly labelled as cooking pears. They are the wrong shape for that. So we must fall back on the first definition, which seems admirable to me.

As the amateurs in the team, they keep us professionals up to scratch. As good all-rounders they take a big share in both the batting and bowling, and it is hard to imagine how we could manage without them.

Ladies and gentlemen, I ask you to give a hearty response to the toast of the churchwardens.

## Useful quotations

You can only make others better by being good yourself. – *Hawers*

We can all be angry with our neighbour. What we want is to be shown, not his defects, of which we are too conscious, but his merits, to which we are too blind. – *R.L. Stevenson*

There can hardly, I believe, be imagined a more desirable pleasure than that of praise unmixed with any possibility of flattery. – *Sir Richard Steele*

He had only vanity: he thought he could give advice better than any other person. – *Mark Twain*

*See also under* The Bishop.

# Reply to the Toast of the Churchwardens

This speech, made by one of the churchwardens, is largely governed by what was said by the proposer of the toast. Generally speaking, however, it will consist of a modest disavowal of the kind things said by the previous speaker and an expression of pleasure in the duties of the churchwarden. This speech needs humour.

## Specimen

Ladies and gentlemen – our Vicar has said some very kind things about the churchwardens, and he has put me in a very difficult position. If I accept all these compliments without demur, I shall not only be lacking in modesty, but also guilty of suppressing the truth. If, on the other hand, I deny the justice of his remarks, I shall be suggesting that the Vicar himself has not been speaking the truth. Now you all know that the Vicar is the most honest of men, and must therefore be puzzled to know how he can have come to say such nice things about people who have done little to deserve them.

The fact of the matter is simply that the Vicar has a happy habit of seeing the good in the worst of us. He showed this to me quite clearly the other day when we made a train journey together. According to the timetable we should have arrived at our destination just in time for lunch, but in fact we still had a fair way to go when lunchtime arrived. I put this down to the inefficiency of the railway, but the Vicar's opinion was that he must have made a mistake in reading the timetable. The train stopped at a station, and we learned that it was unlikely to remain there for more than a minute or so. We decided that there was no time even for a dash to the buffet. However, a rather grimy little boy was standing on the platform and the Vicar beckoned to him.

'Here's £1,' he said. ' Now please go to the buffet and buy three doughnuts, and bring back two for my friend and myself. The other one is for you.' The boy seized the coin and dashed off to the buffet.

'I don't think we'll see him again,' I said, 'or your pound.' The Vicar chided me gently for my lack of faith in human nature.

'He'll come back,' he said confidently. And I knew it was useless to argue, because even if the boy didn't come back the Vicar would have found some excuse for him.

As it happened, however, the boy did return, with a doughnut wedged firmly in his mouth. But that was the only one he had, and when he reached the window of our carriage he thrust some change into the Vicar's hand.

'Sorry,' he mumbled. 'They only had one left.'

And then the Vicar thanked him gravely and turned to me and said,

'You see? I told you he was an honest lad.'

And that story, I think, explains why you have heard things about the churchwardens that must differ greatly from your own knowledge of us. Ladies and gentlemen, on behalf of my colleagues, I thank you.

# CHAPTER EIGHT

# The School

## Speech Day: Presentation of the Prizes

The speaker must remember that a large part of the audience consists of youngsters, and should adapt the speech accordingly without patronising. Above all the audience shouldn't be told that schooldays are 'the happiest days of your life'.

### *Specimen*

Ladies and gentlemen – A few moments ago, while I was sitting on this platform, feeling sorry for myself because I had to make a speech, my thoughts went back to the last speech day I attended. It was, in fact, my last speech day at school. I remember it very well, because I happened to win a prize – the only prize I ever won all the time I was at school.

On that occasion a very distinguished gentleman came to the school to present the prizes. Nowadays, of course, this job is done by very undistinguished people. This gentleman followed the custom and made a speech, and I shall never forget what he said. You see, I was feeling rather pleased with myself, because I had won this prize and my parents were there to see me go up to collect it. And I thought the speaker was going to say what a fine thing it was to win a prize.

But he did not say that. He told us about his schooldays, just as I am telling you about mine. And he told us that he had never won a prize. While congratulating the prize-winners, he stressed that just because you win a prize at school doesn't mean you will automatically go on to be a success in everything you do. In fact, those who go away empty-handed on these occasions are just as likely to be achievers in life, while there is no guarantee that prize-winners will not fall by the wayside at some point.

Now I am not going to make a speech like that. In fact, I am not going to make a speech at all. I am just going to present the prizes, and I want to say to the winners now that I offer them my hearty congratulations. I don't think any of them will fall by the wayside, and they have every right to be proud of their success. I will agree that winning prizes at school does not mean that you are bound to make a success of life, any more than not winning prizes means that you are going to be a failure. But let us give credit to those who do.

*(Presentation of the prizes should follow.)*

## Sports Day: Presentation of Cups and Awards

*See under* Speech Day.

### *Specimen*

Ladies and gentlemen – Before I present the prizes, I am expected to make a speech. You probably think that is hard on you, but I assure you that it is much harder on me. So for my sake as well as yours, it is going to be short.

I have seen a magnificent display of athletics today. And when I say magnificent, I am not referring only to the time-keeper's records, although these reveal some pretty fine achievements. But the really fine thing was the spirit shown by the competitors – by all the competitors and not only those who won prizes.

I do not want to belittle the victors. You have heard it said that we should count the game above the prize – and so we should; but that does not mean that the prize is of no value. Our first congratulations go to the winners, who have every right to be proud of their achievements. But we must also congratulate all the other competitors. Not because they lost – but because they did their best and what fine, courageous efforts they were.

So congratulations to you all – but especially to the winners.

*(Presentation of the prizes should follow.)*

# Vote of Thanks after a School Concert or Play

This speech is usually made by a parent. Follow the suggestions made under Speech Day and Vote of Thanks to an Amateur Dramatic Society.

## *Specimen*

Ladies and gentlemen – A few days ago I was asked if I would propose a vote of thanks after the school concert. That seemed to me almost as bad a task as having to get up on the stage and do a turn myself; so I sat down and after a lot of labour I managed to write out a speech. Then I learned it by heart, and that was harder than learning Shakespeare. And now I cannot make the speech at all because it would sound absurd after a concert such as this. I expected it to be good, but I never thought it could be as good as it has been.

My own memory of school concerts is rather dim, but I know we never put on shows of this class. Acting, singing, dancing – everything has been of the highest quality. You have given us a show that would shame most shows in the West End of London. I am not going to single out any particular item in the programme because it was all so good. And so, to all of those who worked behind the scenes as well as those who entertained us from behind the footlights, I offer the appreciation and gratitude of the audience. Thank you all very much.

# The School Chaplain

*See under* Speech Day and The Vicar.

## Specimen

Ladies and gentlemen – There are three good reasons why my speech should be brief. One is that I don't like speaking; another is, no doubt, that you don't like listening to me. But the most important reason is that our Chaplain is far too modest to enjoy hearing anyone sing his praises. He has done so much for the school that it would be poor return to embarrass him with an appreciation which could not do him justice anyway.

A school chaplain, like an army padre, has to be a very special sort of minister. All the clergy must know how to preach, but the chaplain and the padre must also know how not to preach. Our chaplain has both qualifications and uses them with excellent skill and proper timing. Not only is he an inspiration to the whole school, but he is the personal friend of every single pupil.

Ladies and gentlemen, I give you the toast of our chaplain.

## Useful quotations

I am no orator, as Brutus is;
But, as you know me all, a plain blunt man. – *William Shakespeare*

*See also under* The Bishop.

# School Reunion

This toast is proposed by a former pupil, and it should be quite brief and simple.

## Specimen

Ladies (and/or Gentlemen) – The Old School Tie has been the subject of so many music hall jokes that one might expect it to have been laughed out of existence. Yet there seems to be plenty of evidence to the contrary here tonight; and the fact that it has survived so much ridicule proves that it is by no means a meaningless symbol.

Most loyalties are difficult to explain, and loyalty to the school is no exception. Old Boys' or Old Girls' Associations differ from most other societies in one important respect: their members are not proposed and elected, and indeed have little say in the matter of qualification for membership. The only thing that we have in common, on the face of it, is that our respective parents happened to send us to the same school; and one might ask what bond can exist among us. The answer is simple. As pupils we were drawn together in comradeship, not because we liked the look of each other's faces – I am sure you will agree with me on this point – but through loyalty to a common ideal.

The strength of that ideal lies in the fact that it continues to hold us together after the end of our communal life. It is not easy to express its source of inspiration. It has nothing to do with the school's scholastic or sporting achievements; it does not derive from the buildings or grounds; it does not even come from the head and the teaching staff – saving their presence – although without their good influence it could hardly survive. It is simply one of those imponderables, and can only be defined as the spirit of the school – a spirit compounded of honour, teamwork, comradeship and all that is best in communal life.

Ladies and gentlemen – The School!

## *Useful quotations*

The future is purchased by the present. – *Dr Johnson*

A true and noble friendship shrinks not at the greatest of trials. – *Jeremy Taylor*

When men are friends, there is no need of justice; but when they are just, they still need friendship. – *Aristotle*

The belongings of friends are common. – *Aristotle*

Sweet is the remembrance of troubles when you are in safety. – *Euripides*

# CHAPTER NINE

# Political and Electoral

## Introducing the Candidate
## at an Election Meeting

This speech is made by the chairperson. The difficulty in making a speech involving political considerations is not so much in the subject matter as in handling the audience. When you make a social speech or propose a convivial toast, you will generally find that your listeners will meet you in a friendly spirit; but whenever you have to touch on politics in public, you may be sure that at least a section of your audience will be hostile, and probably vocally so. Some general advice on dealing with hecklers has been given in Chapter 3 Delivering a Speech, and in preparing your speech you must keep this danger well in mind. Don't include anything that will provoke awkward questions or facetious remarks.

In introducing a candidate you are not expected to go into details of his or her policy – that is the candidate's task. But your speech is important, because if it is properly prepared and delivered you can put the audience into a receptive mood. Naturally your speech should be largely personal, but do not make the mistake of giving the candidate extravagant praise, which might provoke derision and cause embarrassment.

## *Specimen*

L adies and gentlemen – As chairman of this meeting I
have the pleasure of introducing — as a candidate to
represent the interests of this borough in parliament. As
you know, she is the representative of the — Party; and
you will have guessed, if you did not already know, that I
too am a supporter of that party. I believe in its principles
and its policies, and I am convinced that if it is returned
to power at the election – as I am sure it will be – every
member of the community will benefit.

But I am not going to talk politics or try to anticipate
our candidate's speech. You have come to hear her and I
am not going to waste your time with a long introduction.
All I want to say is that — is, in my opinion, admirably
fitted to represent this borough, not only because her
politics are sound but also because she has great integrity
and ability. I commend her to you and I trust you will give
her the good hearing she deserves.

# Introducing the Candidate
# at a Municipal Election Meeting

This speech is made by the chairperson. *See under* Introducing the Candidate at an Election Meeting.

Note also that this speech can be more personal and should
include brief reference to topical local affairs. The subject
matter of the speech will depend on whether the candidate
represents the party that had a majority before the election or
whether he or she belongs to the present Opposition. If the
former, the audience will need to be reminded of the work
done; if the latter, the speech should be more critical of the
present state of affairs. Again, however, the speaker should not
try to anticipate what the candidate has to say.

## *Specimen*

L adies and gentlemen – As chairman of this meeting I
have the pleasure of introducing — as a candidate for
election to the Town Council. For good or bad, candidates
for municipal elections, like general elections, have to
fight under party labels. You know —'s label, and you will
have deduced that she has already been promised my

support and my vote. But I ask you to regard her as something more than a good party member. She has, I know, the very real interests of our town at heart, and has both the energy and the ability to play an important part on our council.

I am not going to give you my own opinions on the present state of local politics, nor shall I pass any judgment on what has been done – or what has not been done – by the last council. Each elector will make his or her own mind up on that when recording his or her vote. But I feel bound to remind you that there are number of local problems that urgently need to be solved, and the next council, however it is composed, will fail in its duty unless it tackles these with courage and resolution. There is, for example, the matter of (insert a reference to a topical local issue on which the candidate is taking a strong line). This problem is not new, and it must be apparent that it is unlikely to be solved unless we have a council that is prepared to tackle it vigorously. — has, I know, strong views on this and other pressing matters which you are about to hear. I think she will satisfy you that her views are sound as well as strong; and I am convinced that she will make it quite clear that she has the energy and drive necessary to put them into practice. We need people of energy and drive on our council.

Ladies and gentlemen, your candidate —.

## *Useful quotations*

He served his party best, who serves the country best. – *R.B. Hayes*

Can anybody remember when times were not hard and money not scarce? – *Ralph Waldo Emerson*

We cannot eat the fruit while the tree is in blossom. – *Benjamin Disraeli*

Work is the greatest cure of all maladies and miseries that ever beset mankind. – *Thomas Carlyle*

There's dignity in labour. – *Swain*

# Proposing the Adoption of a Candidate for an Election

Candidates for elections are adopted at meetings of the local party, so here the issue is more personal than political. However, a candidate is adopted more for political ability than for personal qualities, and the speaker who proposes the adoption should base his or her case on this.

## *Specimen*

Mr Chairman (or Madam Chair), ladies and gentlemen. I have the agreeable task of proposing the adoption of — as our candidate for the coming general election. I am not going to support my proposal by drawing from my personal knowledge of — , because the matter is too important for sentiment. We are all agreed that it is our task to choose the best possible candidate – that is, the candidate most likely to win the election and to represent us in the way we would wish after election. I think that — is entirely suitable on both counts. He has been frank about his opinions on those points in the party programme that concern us most, and I think you will agree that his views are entirely sound. He is a person of considerable political knowledge and experience, and he has that high degree of common sense necessary for a politician in dealing with those problems and issues that inevitably arise after the election is over.

You all know that this is by no means an easy constituency, and only a strong candidate can have any hope of winning. I think that — has just the qualities that will appeal to the electorate. His public record is excellent, he has a most pleasant personality, he is an excellent speaker, and impresses people as a person who will get things done. And I am sure that when he is elected he will get them done, too. It is therefore with every confidence that I propose that — should be formally adopted as our candidate.

# Opposing the Adoption of a Candidate for an Election

Frankness is essential here, of course; but it should not exceed the bounds of courtesy and decency. There must be no hint of personal abuse.

## *Specimen*

Mr Chairman (or Madam Chair), ladies and gentlemen. It is with very great regret that I have to oppose the recommendation to adopt — as our candidate for the next election. I must make it clear from the start that my opposition is in no way personal. I respect — for his integrity and sincerity, and I am sure that if he were adopted he would not spare himself in trying to prove worthy of our trust; and that, if he were elected, he would make equally strenuous efforts to represent this constituency in a proper way.

But the matter is far too serious for good intentions to be accepted by themselves. Frankly, I do not think — is suitable to represent either the party or the constituency. He has been very frank in giving opinions on various aspects of the party programme, but on many points he does not appear to have understood all the implications. In particular, there is his attitude on the matter of (insert some appropriate matter). His replies to various questions on this subject have been, to say the least, meagre and vague. I will not say they were deliberately evasive, because I am sure they were not; but I suggest to you that this is a question of vital importance to us as electors, and — does not appear to have grasped its importance at all.

There are other matters on which —'s views appear to be in conflict with our own. One is (insert appropriate matter). You will remember at previous meetings we have passed resolutions strongly in favour of this. The last occasion when we expressed this opinion was only three months ago. —, however, seems inclined to take a different view. Another point on which we are agreed is the matter of (insert appropriate matter). On this — does not seem to have taken up a very definite position, but the little he has said does not appear to me to be in agreement with our own opinions.

What concerns me especially is that these issues, which — treats rather casually, are bound to be raised by the other side in the coming election campaign. They need to be faced by someone who understands the problems and appreciates our conception of how they can be solved. I am well aware that from a national point of view the election will be fought on much broader lines; but you know that the people of this constituency are keenly interested in our local problems, and I am convinced that the way these are handled by our candidate will decide the fate of many votes, if not the actual results of the poll.

I have no doubt that — is a loyal member of the party, and that he has the general ability to make an excellent Member of Parliament. But I do not think this is the right constituency for him. I am not making this criticism merely because he is not a local man; but I think he is unsuitable because he neither understands nor appreciates the importance of issues peculiar to this constituency which will be widely discussed during the election, and which will need to be brought to the attention of the government – whatever the government is – when the election is over.

For these reasons I feel bound to oppose the adoption of — as your candidate.

## *Useful quotations*

Remember what Simonides said – that he never repented that he had held his tongue, but often that he had spoken. – *Plutarch*

Better not do the deed than weep it done.
– *Matthew Prior*

Good rarely came from good advice. – *Lord Byron*

Advice is seldom welcome, and those who want it the most always like it the least. – *Lord Chesterfield*

# Our Member of Parliament

The toast to the local MP may be proposed at a purely party gathering or at a function where the audience is more general. In the latter case the speaker should steer clear of political controversy, for the toast itself should be readily acceptable to the whole audience.

## *Specimen*

Ladies and gentlemen – It is with great pleasure that I rise to propose the toast of our Member of Parliament. This is not a political function, and I am not going to make a political speech. Indeed, I am not going to make a speech at all, for I am sure that after the last stormy session at Westminster, — has heard enough speeches to last him until the end of the recess. All I want to say today is this.

Whatever our Member has said in the House of Commons – and he may be surprised to know how closely we read his speeches – he has never forgotten the interests of his constituents. On several occasions he has spoken up on our behalf, even at the risk of making himself unpopular with the party to which he belongs; and ever since he was elected he has, I know, personally investigated every request and complaint that he has received from a constituent. His presence with us today is one more example of his concern with local affairs; and when he next presents himself to the electorate, whether we put him in again or cast him into the political wilderness, he may rest assured that the efforts he has made on our behalf as a community will have been both recognised and appreciated.

Ladies and gentlemen, I give you the toast of our MP, —.

## *Useful quotations*

*See under* Introducing the Candidate at a Municipal Election Meeting and Opposing the Adoption of a Candidate for an Election.

# CHAPTER TEN

# Social Toasts

## The Ladies

This toast is usually proposed by the youngest bachelor in the company, and the spirit of this choice should be reflected in his speech. It should be light-hearted but, of course, flattering to the fair sex. Humour is naturally desirable, but the speaker should exercise particular care to ensure that his jokes are in good taste. If a joke seems only a shade doubtful, it is better to leave it out.

### *Specimen*

Gentlemen – The task of proposing this toast has been given to me because I happen to be the youngest bachelor here tonight. I do not know the origin of this custom, but I image it must be because the youngest is the least likely to be a confirmed bachelor, and his single state is probably not due to any lack of appreciation of the opposite sex. In my own case I may as well admit that I am full of appreciation. The ladies here tonight have only a poor speaker to extol their charms, but they could not find a more devoted admirer.

I hope you will not think that because I am single, I know nothing about the ladies. I haven't, of course, had the same concentrated experience as a married man, but no doubt that will come later. Meanwhile I am steadily enlarging my knowledge of the fair sex in general – at least, to the extent that they will allow me. And every enlargement of my knowledge adds still further to my admiration.

We sometimes hear talk, even in these modern times, of the so-called equality of women, as though it were something to be argued about. I am neither a social historian nor a prophet, but I venture to suggest that such a thing as equality has never existed and never will exist. Women have never been our equals: they have always been vastly superior to us. There might be more sense in talking about equality for men!

I ask you to join me in drinking to their health. Gentlemen – the Ladies!

### Useful quotations

Nature intended that women should be her masterpiece. – *Doris Lessing*

O woman, lovely women, nature made thee.
To temper man; we had been brutes without you. – *Thomas Otway*

I for one venerate a petticoat. – *Lord Byron*

The most beautiful object in the world, it will be allowed, is a beautiful woman. – *Lord Macaulay*

Man has his will; but woman has her way. – *O.W. Holes*

## Reply to the Toast of the Ladies

### Specimen

Gentlemen – My difficulty in replying to your most generous toast is that I am not allowed to say what I want to. You are allowed to flatter us as much as you like – and almost as much as we like – but the only times when we are allowed to tell you what we think of you are when our thoughts are unfriendly. The primmest Victorian miss always had the right to say to a man, 'Sir,

your attentions are unwelcome. Pray desist.' But today, for
all our much-vaunted freedom, no girl would dare to say
to a man, 'Sir, your attentions are very welcome. Please
carry on.' That would be regarded as immodest, if not
worse. All women are expected to have a natural modesty,
but, however, I suspect that the Frenchman Balzac got
nearer the truth when he said, 'Woman's modesty is
man's greatest invention.'

So here I am, allowed to say no more than thank you
for the very kind compliments you have paid us. I dare
not tell you in reply that I have been an admirer of men
almost from the cradle; that I find you good to look at,
pleasant to listen to, delightful to dance with, charming
companions; that, in fact, I think you are wonderful!
These are the things I dare not say – but perhaps now you
will be able to guess them.

### Useful quotations

Woman will be last thing civilised by man. – *George Meredith*

A woman is only a woman, but a good cigar is a smoke. – *Rudyard Kipling*

## Our Guests

The specimen given below will need to be adapted to the
nature of the function and especially to the guests who have
been invited to attend. The proposer should include in his
speech some complimentary allusions to the more prominent
guests – including, of course, the guest who has been chosen
to reply to the toast.

### Specimen

Ladies and gentlemen – It is my privilege to propose the
health of our guests. It is an easy task, and requires
few words and no formality from me; for most of our
guests are not strangers. I hope that by the time they leave
they will all think of themselves as our friends.

Some of our guests have travelled quite a long way to be
with us tonight, and I know I am expressing the general

opinion when I say how much we appreciate the compliment they have paid us in spending the evening with us. I only hope that they will not regret their kindness. I am reminded of a story about George Bernard Shaw. He was a guest at a social function and was asked afterwards what the company was like. 'Terrible,' he replied. 'I should have been bored stiff if I hadn't been there.' I hope none of our guests will think this worth quoting when asked the same question.

We are pleased to see with us (insert the allusions to prominent guests).

Finally I want to say how much pleasure the presence of all our guests has given us, and to express the hope that we shall have many opportunities of seeing more of them in the future and getting to know them better.

Ladies and gentlemen, I give you the toast of – Our Guests!

## Reply to the Toast of Our Guests

### *Specimen*

Ladies and gentlemen – When a man has been wined and dined in this regal fashion, his only concern is whether he can manage to get up on his feet and stay there long enough to express his thanks. I have, as you see, achieved the first part of this task; and the length of my speech will depend on how far I can carry out the second part. I can safely promise you that my subsidence will not be delayed for very long.

To thank you for your magnificent hospitality would be hard enough by itself, but you have made my task even harder. You have actually thanked us for coming here and enjoying that hospitality. You have even gone so far so to drink to our health, after you have done everything you could to undermine it! I can think of only one reply to your generous toast. Whatever difficulties we are going to have in getting home, we had none in getting here. There was absolutely no inconvenience to any of us. If we really earned your thanks by coming here – and it seems very difficult to believe – then we are ready to confer the same favour again as many times as you like!

Ladies and gentlemen, on behalf of the guests, I offer you my warmest thanks for this most enjoyable evening.

## Absent Friends

This speech should be short and sincere. Humour is best avoided, as flippancy is in bad taste. The specimen below needs to be adopted to suit the circumstances.

### *Specimen*

Ladies and gentlemen – You do not want a long speech to introduce this toast. It is a simple toast, with a wealth of meaning. Most of us have family and friends a long way away whom we wish were with us now. Their presence would add to the enjoyment of our festivities. But I am sure that they would want us to enjoy ourselves just as much in their absence, and would ask no more than that we should make a brief pause to think quietly of them for a few moments, and drink in silence to – Absent Friends.

### *Useful quotations*

No speech ever uttered or utterable is worth comparison with silence. – *Thomas Carlyle*

Absent in body, but present in spirit. – *I Corinthians*

## The Bride and the Bridegroom

This toast, which is usually proposed by the bride's father or an old friend of the bride, should be brief and tactful. The proposer should remember that the bride and groom are probably embarrassed and he should not try to get cheap laughs at their expense.

### *Specimen*

Ladies and gentlemen – I have a happy duty to perform on this happy occasion. I am going to ask you all to drink to the health and happiness of the bride and groom. It is an especially happy task because I can perform it wish such confidence. Both of them look the picture of health and their happiness is beyond concealment.

Marriage has sometimes been called a lottery, but I am sure there is no gamble about this match. Both the bride and groom took a peek in advance at the winning numbers before they chose their tickets. Of course I could have told the groom that he had found winner right from the start, for I have known the bride since she was a sweet and lovable child, and watched her become sweeter and more lovable as she grew up. But the groom wisely did not ask my opinion, and nor did the bride. I hope they will forgive me if I give it now.

No one forgets their wedding day, and this young couple will look back on this day with precious memories as the years pass. I doubt if their memories will include my speech, so I will simply ask you to drink to the health and happiness of the bride and groom.

## *Useful quotations*

Marriage is a great institution. But who wants to live in an institution. – *Groucho Marx*

Of all the actions of a man's life, his marriage does least concern other people; yet of all actions of our life 'tis most meddled with by other people. – *Table talk*

No woman should marry a teetotaller, or a man who does not smoke. – *R.L. Stevenson*

## Reply to the Toast of the Bride and the Bridegroom

This speech, which is traditionally made by the bridegroom, can be very brief. No one expects a flow of oratory from a man who has just got married, and it is enough if he simply voices his thanks. Should he want to make a longer speech, he will naturally say how fortunate he considers himself, but he should not give a long list of the bride's qualities; nor should he forget to mention his appreciation of the kindness shown to him by her parents. The bridegroom's speech usually ends with the toast of the bridesmaids.

## *Specimen*

Ladies and gentlemen – My wife and I – I must get used to this way of speaking – thank you all most sincerely for your kind wishes. I am sure you will excuse me from making a long speech, and will understand that at the moment I am quite incapable of making one. I don't need to tell you that I think I am the luckiest man in the world, and that my only ambition is to be worthy of my luck. I must add that today I have not only gained the best wife any man could have, but I have also acquired an extra mother and father. No parents could have been kinder to a man bent on stealing their daughter.

Before I sit down, I must ask you to join me in drinking to the health of the very charming ladies who have supported my wife in her ordeal – if that is the right word. Ladies and gentlemen – to the bridesmaids!

### *Useful quotations*

The most precious possession that ever comes to a man in this world is a woman's heart. – *Holland*

Let him now speak, or else hereafter for ever hold his peace. – *Book of Common Prayer*

## The Bridesmaids

Usually the proposal of this toast is included in the bridegroom's reply to the toast of the bride and bridegroom (see above). It need only be short but should be light and complimentary and never cause embarrassment.

### *Specimen*

Ladies and gentlemen – I hope that the only two really important people here will not mind if I distract your thoughts from them for a moment. Possibly they will even welcome a brief escape from the limelight; and I am sure they will agree that the subjects of my toast are well worth your attention. I mean, of course, the bridesmaids. The bride has told me that they have given her no end of help, and my own eyes tell me that their decorative value has greatly helped the success of the day. They have performed their duties so charmingly that I might be tempted to say that they should always be bridesmaids – but they are far too charming to have much chance of that!

Ladies and gentlemen – to the bridesmaids!

### Useful quotations

I have always thought that every woman should marry, and no man. – *Benjamin Disraeli*

The hardest task in a girl's life is to prove to a man that his intentions are serious. – *Helen Rowland*

*See also under* The Ladies.

## Reply to the Toast of the Bridesmaids

This speech is invariably made by the best man, and again tact is essential. The recent trend towards a jovial best man's speech, usually at the expense of the groom, does not form part of the formal toasting.

### Specimen

Ladies and gentlemen – May I on behalf of the bridesmaids thank you for those kind remarks, while at the same time adding my own thanks for the way they have carried out their duties so beautifully. The role of bridesmaid is an important one, but I'm sure they will not mind my saying that it is not an arduous task. It is an honour and a pleasure to support a friend on this wonderful occasion and to take part in such a joyful ceremony. From the bridesmaids, thank you all.

# The Baby at a Christening or Naming Party

This toast is invariably proposed by the baby's godfather or a family friend. It should be light-hearted and cheerful in character, and include a compliment to the mother and father. If the godfather is a grandfather, he can recall an anecdote about the mother or father as a baby.

## *Specimen*

Ladies and gentlemen – I have the greatest pleasure in proposing the health of our robust-looking guest of honour. This is his first real public appearance, and I am sure you will agree that he has made a big success of it. It is perhaps a little too early to discuss his character, but certainly he has already won all our hearts. Of course he ought to be a fine baby, because he has the finest start in life any baby can have: good parents. We know that they will give him all the love and care needed to make his childhood happy; and I am sure that he, in his turn, will give great joy to them. So I ask you to drink to the health of —, and may he have a long and happy life.

## *Useful quotations*

Every baby born into the world is a finer one than the last. – *Charles Dickens*

Children are the last word of human imperfection. They cry, my dear; they put vexatious questions; they demand to be fed, to be washed, to be educated, to have their noses blowed; and when the time comes, they break our hearts, as I break this piece of sugar. – *R.L. Stevenson*

In general those parents have the most reverence who most deserve it. – *Dr Johnson*

# Reply to the Toast of the Baby

This toast is usually made by the baby's father, and should include reference to the godparents if there are any.

## *Specimen*

Ladies and gentlemen – I must apologise on behalf of my son, who regrets that he is unable to reply to your kind toast himself. He has asked me to do the job for him. This is not the worst job I have had to do for him in his short life, and I do not doubt that harder tasks lie in store.

My wife and I are grateful to you for the very kind and flattering things you have said about us, which we do not deserve. We may be very ordinary parents – but I hope you will pardon me if I point out that, in my opinion, our child is no ordinary baby.

We want to thank you all for coming to give — your support on this important occasion of his life, and our special thanks are due to those who have kindly acted as his sponsors. May I ask you to drink their health, too? Ladies and gentlemen, to our baby's godparents.

## A Birthday Toast

The character of this speech will naturally depend greatly on the age of the person whose birthday is being celebrated. The toast is usually proposed by an old friend, who is allowed to relate some humorous anecdotes drawn from the friendship. While the proposer will naturally point out some of the good qualities of his or her friend, fulsome praise should be avoided or embarrassment might be caused, and the plaudits might appear insincere.

## *Specimen*

Ladies and gentlemen – I have been asked to propose this toast because I am —'s oldest friend. I am not sure if this does him justice. An old saying tells us that a man should be judged by his choice of friends, and I should hate to think that —'s reputation was linked too closely to mine. I think I can say that it is only in this matter of choosing friends that I have better taste than he has.

But it is not merely for his good taste that — deserves our good wishes. I am not going to embarrass him by reciting a catalogue of his many fine qualities, but I think he will forgive me if I tell you of just one little experience that we shared many years ago. (Describe an incident to the credit of the subject of the toast.)

So, ladies and gentlemen, I ask you to join me in drinking the health of —, and in wishing him many happy returns. May he have many more birthdays to come!

## Useful quotations

A faithful friend is the medicine of life. – *Apochrypha*

They are rich who have true friends. – *Thomas Fuller*

The ornament of a house is the friends who frequent it. – *Ralph Waldo Emerson*

A friend may well be reckoned the masterpiece of nature. – *Ralph Waldo Emerson*

If he have not a friend, he may quit the stage. – *Francis Bacon*

Be slow in choosing a friend, slow in changing. – *Benjamin Franklin*

The highest friendship must always lead us to the highest pleasure. – *Henry Fielding*

Friendship is the gift of the gods, and the most precious boon to man. – *Benjamin Disraeli*

# Reply to a Birthday Toast

Express surprise about all the good things said to you, and do not add to them. Be brief.

## Specimen

Ladies and gentlemen – — has done me many acts of friendship in the past, and I have always appreciated them; but today, I think, he has been much too kind and not very truthful. He has credited me with virtues I have never possessed, and conveniently forgotten all my many failings. I am not going to correct him, because if I did you would start doubting whether any friend of mine could be as fine a man as you know — to be. The fact is that I am lucky in my friends, and the proof of my good fortune is in the company that has honoured me by coming here today. There is an old saying, 'Be sure your friends will find you out.' I don't believe it, for my friends have never found me out, and I hope they never do. Ladies and gentlemen, thank you very much indeed for all your kind wishes.

# At a Coming of Age of a Man

After the proposing of the toast, it might be appropriate to lead a chorus of 'For he's a jolly good fellow'. *See also under* A Birthday Toast.

## *Specimen*

Ladies and gentlemen – It is my very pleasant duty to propose the health of — on reaching his majority. I will not use the expression 'coming of age' because frankly I dislike it. If age comes at 18, then I must have died years ago. And how can you think of age when you look at our young friend? To me he represents the coming of youth. He is old only in the sense that he has now reached the age when most people stop wanting to be older. Happily he has a good many years to enjoy before he will reach the age when he will start to want to be younger.

Some people never grow up, and others are old for their age. I hope that — will take it as compliment when I express the opinion that he seems to me to be absolutely 18 in every respect. I am not going to embarrass him by reciting a catalogue of his many fine qualities, nor am I going to bore him with the advice of an old man, which he would probably ignore anyway. I think it was Somerset Maugham who said that there is a sort of conspiracy among older folks to pretend that they are wiser than younger folks, and the younger folks do not rumble it until they themselves have got older – and then, of course, it pays them to join in the conspiracy!

I am sure that — will live a happy, successful and useful life, for he has all the qualities necessary for this enviable trinity. So ladies and gentlemen, I give you this toast. To our good friend —.

## *Alternative specimen*

This version is more suitable when the proposer is an older man and an intimate friend of the family.

Ladies and gentlemen – No one could have more pleasure than I in proposing the health of — on this important occasion. I have known him for a long time – longer, indeed than he has known me; for when I first set eyes on him he was an infant in his mother's arms. I shall not embarrass him by recalling my memories of the first of his seven ages, although it is only fair to say that I have no recollection of him either mewling or puking. Nor, as a schoolboy, did he ever whine.

The first two of his seven ages are past now, and according to Shakespeare we shall next see him as a lover:

*Sighing like furnace, with a woeful ballad*
*Made to his mistress' eyebrow.*

It is not an easy picture to imagine. I have rarely heard — sigh, and never like a furnace. If he has poetic talent he has kept it well hidden, and I am sure his ballads would be anything but woeful. And in any case, ladies' eyebrows are not what they were in Shakespeare's day. But I have no doubt that — will make – if has not already made – speedy conquests of the hearts of the ladies, for his good qualities are quite exceptional. Nor do I doubt that his life will continue to be happy, successful, and useful. So I ask you to drink to the health of —.

## *Useful quotations*

The youth of a nation are the trustees of posterity. – *Benjamin Disraeli*

They can conquer who believe they can. – *Ralph Waldo Emerson*

A wise man makes more opportunities than he finds. – *Francis Bacon*

If youth be a defect, it is one that we outgrow only too soon. – *J.R. Lovell*

# Reply to a Coming of Age Toast to a Man

*See under* Reply to a Birthday Toast.

## *Specimen*

Ladies and gentlemen – I have heard it said that young men think older men fools, and that older men *know* young men to be so. One day I shall learn how true the second part of the saying is; I hope it is not entirely accurate because I can say quite honestly that I do not hold with the first part. For the moment I must express my thanks for the honour you have paid me on this rather important occasion. I must also thank you very much for not asking me how it feels to be 18, because of course it feels just the same as 17.

I am not going to attempt to reply to the compliments you have paid me, which are entirely undeserved; but I feel bound to say one thing. Whatever advantages I have in life I owe entirely to my mother and father. If I succeed in anything, it is thanks largely to them. If I fail, the fault lies with myself. If I can live up to their standards I shall consider myself a lucky man. Once again, thank you very much.

# At a Coming of Age of a Woman

*See under* A Birthday Toast.

## *Specimen*

Ladies and gentlemen – My task tonight is an honour rather than a duty, for I am sure that I am generally envied for being chosen to propose the health of — on her eighteenth birthday. My only qualification is that I have had the privilege of wishing her many happy returns on most of her other birthdays. I can even remember her first birthday, when I took her in my arms, and later occasions when she sat on my knee. You will, I am sure, appreciate that I recall these rather wistfully, for I am unlikely to get any further opportunities of this nature.

I have watched — grow up. I have seen childish prettiness give way to womanly beauty; I have seen good nature broaden into charm. To me she has always been sweet and lovable, and I am sure she will remain the same for the rest of her life. Ladies and gentlemen, I ask you to join me in drinking the health of — and wishing her many happy returns on her eighteenth birthday.

### Useful quotations
*See* At a Coming of Age of a Man and The Ladies

# Reply to a Coming of Age Toast to a Woman

No formal speech is required. All that the lady is expected to do is to get up and voice her thanks in her own words.

## Specimen

Ladies and gentlemen – Thank you very much for those kind words. I am quite overwhelmed. I don't want to make a speech, but I should just like to thank you for coming to share this special occasion with me and for all the wonderful gifts you have brought. Thank you all.

## At a Silver Wedding Party

The speech, which is usually made by the oldest friend of the married couple, should be quiet and sincere. It can of course be adapted for use on other key anniversaries.

## Specimen

Ladies and gentlemen – I can almost say that I have looked forward to this moment for 25 years, because I was present at the wedding of the charming couple in whose honour I am speaking tonight. It is sometimes said that a friend who marries is a friend lost, but when — got married I not only retained his friendship, but also gained another friend. For 25 years I have enjoyed the kindness of our host and hostess, and if I can enjoy the same friendship until their wedding turns from silver to gold, then I shall be very happy.

It is, I think, just as well that I am here tonight to vouch for the authenticity of the celebration. Had I not had the proof of my own eyes, I should find it hard to believe that our host and hostess have been married so long. In looks and spirit they are both so much younger than their years; and their obvious delight in each other could not be surpassed by newly-weds. I think it is clear to everyone here that their loving relationship has grown and strengthened over the years, and looks set to continue in that vein for the rest of their lives together.

Let us drink to their health, and wish them as much happiness together in the future as they have had in the past. They could not have more. Ladies and gentlemen, to Mr and Mrs —.

## Useful quotations

Well-married, a man is winged; ill-matched, he is shackled. – *Beecher*

Many, being reasonable, must get drunk;
The best of life is but intoxication. – *Lord Byron*

*See also under* The Bride and Bridegroom.

# Reply to a Silver Wedding Toast

This reply is usually made by the husband.

## Specimen

Ladies and gentlemen – I have been looking forward to this opportunity of expressing the thanks of my wife and myself for your kind wishes and many charming gifts to mark this occasion in our married life. Now you have placed us further in your debt by your most generous response to this toast, and made my task more difficult than ever. Indeed, I can recall only one other occasion in my life when I had to get up and try to express feelings that could not be done full justice by any words. That occasion was exactly 25 years ago today. All I could manage to stammer out then was that I thought I was the luckiest man in the world; and all I can stammer out now is that I know I am the luckiest man in the world.

For 25 years I have enjoyed life with the perfect wife, while she has suffered a husband imperfect in all save one thing: his love for her. We have been happy together, and I think we should have been happy on a desert island; but we have not lived apart from the world, and a good deal of our happiness has been brought to us by our friends. Tonight those friends are with us. And so we thank you all, not only for your kind wishes and presents, but also for the joys you have given us since we were married.

### *Useful quotations*

Is not marriage an open question, when it is alleged, from the beginning of the world, that such as are in the institution wish to get out, and such as are out wish to get in? – *Ralph Waldo Emerson*

Advice to persons about to marry: don't. – *Punch's Almanack*

Strange to say what delight we married people have to see these poor fools decoyed into our condition. – *Samuel Pepys*

## The Spirit of Christmas

Any formal proposal of this toast should be jovial and convivial in keeping with the festivities.

### *Specimen*

Ladies and gentlemen – Christmas, as you all know, is the festival for young children. It is for their sake that we decorate our homes with holly and mistletoe. It is for their sake that we put on paper hats and play jolly games. It is for their sake that we eat turkey and Christmas pudding and a whole variety of other good things. It is for their sake alone – or so we say; and if you believe that, you can believe it is for the sake of the children too, that we drink port and smoke cigars on this occasion.

Please do not think I am decrying the idea that Christmas is primarily a children's feast-day. On the contrary, its great merit is that it makes children of us all. It is the one time in the year when we can forget our grown-up dignity and have a good time, and I ask you to join me in drinking to it.

### Useful quotations

When the turkey's on the table and the candles on the tree, I'm jest about as happy as I ever wanta be.
My children gathered round me an' my neighbours settin' by, I couldn't be no happier, and I don't wanta try.
– *Carolyn Wells*

'God bless us every one,' said Tiny Tim, the last of all.
– *Charles Dickens*

## Happy New Year

The passing of the old year and the coming in of the new may be celebrated with a toast preceded by a brief speech of proposal. The chief point to emphasise is success to those present and to absent friends. Timing is crucial.

### Specimen

Ladies and gentlemen – There is no danger of my detaining you for long, for it is almost midnight. When the clock strikes and the bells ring, I am going to ask you to drink with me to a happy and successful New Year, and to our reunion here in exactly a year's time. As we drink the toast I ask you to spare a thought for absent friends, and let us hope that next year they will be with us. Ladies and gentlemen – the hour is striking – I give you the toast of a Happy New Year!

## Gentlemen's Evening – Opening Remarks

This speech is used when a gentlemen's club is meeting for a social occasion. It can also be used for a formal stag party, perhaps where the groom is an older man. The remarks are made by the chairman and they should be as brief as possible. All that the speaker has to do is to start the ball rolling, welcome any distinguished entertainers, and remind the audience of details of procedure.

## Specimen

Gentlemen – We are here tonight to be entertained, and I happen to know that there is plenty of excellent entertainment in store. My remarks do not come under this heading, but you will be happy to learn that I have already nearly finished my speech. All that remains for me to say is that we are very pleased to welcome — and —, who have kindly come along to amuse us in their own inimitable way. Our other entertainers you already know, and their names are a guarantee of the good things in store. There it is gentlemen. Now I call upon — to open our programme.

## Gentlemen's Evening – Closing Remarks

These remarks are also made by the chairman, and should be equally brief.

## Specimen

Gentlemen – Before we break up this delightful gathering you will, I am sure, want me to express your gratitude to those who have made the evening such a great success. I do not need to comment on the entertainment, because you have already shown your appreciation with noisy enthusiasm. I only want to ask you to be noisy just once more in honour of all the entertainers here tonight.

## Useful quotations

I don't care where the water goes if it doesn't get into the wine. – *G.K. Chesterton*

'It wasn't the wine,' murmured Mr Snodgrass in a broken voice, 'it was the salmon.' – *Charles Dickens*

Intemperance in talk makes a dreadful havoc in the heart. – *Wilson*

# CHAPTER ELEVEN

# *Sporting Toasts*

All the following toasts can be adapted for use by men's or women's teams.

## Our Opponents (Cricket)

Of course sportsmanship is the keynote of this toast, with the emphasis on friendly rivalry and the fact that the game is more important than the result. If your own side has won, make little of the success, mention any luck you may have had, and dwell on the difficulty your team experienced before it could claim the victory. If your side has lost, do not bemoan the absence of your best players or claim that you were unlucky; say that the better team won, and that you hope to get your revenge next time.

Often the convention is for the toast to be proposed by the captain of the winning team and answered by his or her opposite number. However, sometimes the toast is proposed by the captain of the home team, irrespective of the result of the match.

### Specimen

Ladies and/or gentlemen – I have the greatest pleasure in proposing to you the toast of our opponents. I know you will agree with me that we had an excellent game. As it happened, we managed to scrape a win, and on paper it may look a comfortable victory. In fact, as you all know, our opponents gave us some very uncomfortable moments, and the score-board flatters us. Of course I am glad we won, but I am still gladder that we had such a good game. Our opponents were not only keen and able players – their fielding in particular was a lesson to us – but they also showed themselves fine sportsmen. It is not for the result that we shall remember this game so much as the spirit in which it was played. The next time we meet we shall try to win again, although I don't mind admitting that we expect at least as hard a struggle as we had today. But whatever the result, we know in advance that we shall have a good game, played in the spirit in which cricket should always be played.

Gentlemen, I give you to toast of our opponents, the — Club, coupled with the name of their captain, —.

### Useful quotations

Always play fair, and think fair; and if you win, don't crow about it; and if you lose don't fret. – *Eden Phillpotts*

Success is sweet: the sweeter if long delayed and attained through manifold struggles and defeats. – *J.H. Leigh Hunt*

# Reply to the Toast of our Opponents (Cricket)

*See under* Our Opponents (Cricket).

### Specimen

Ladies and/or gentlemen – On behalf of a very chastened team, I wish to thank you for your most cordial toast. We were soundly beaten, and I had no intention of trying to make excuses, but I did not expect to hear excuses made for us. You are too generous in your victory, and I can only reply by saying that the better team won, and we know it. But it is a great comfort to hear that you do not consider your afternoon was entirely wasted, or that you might have done better at the nets. Whatever faults there were in our play – and I know there were plenty – we tried our hardest to give you a good game. The simple fact was that you were too good for us. But we enjoyed the match tremendously, and it is a relief to hear that you got some pleasure out of it.

I must thank you also for the way you have entertained us, providing us with a magnificent tea (and dinner) which we did little to deserve.

According to my memory, a fixture has been arranged for a return match in six weeks' time. Then we shall have the pleasure of offering you our hospitality and, we hope, of avenging today's defeat. It may seen boastful to make this suggestion after our performance today, but like most cricketers we never know when we are beaten, and the next time we take the field against you we shall be more determined than ever. Anyway, whatever the result, I share your knowledge that we are going to have good, sporting game.

On behalf of the — Club, I thank you.

## Our Opponents (Football)

*See under* Our Opponents (Cricket). Both these toasts can be easily adapted for other team sports.

### *Specimen*

Ladies and/or gentlemen – I have great pleasure in asking you to drink the health of our very formidable opponents. We knew in advance that we were in for a hard struggle, and we went on the field determined to play to the best of our ability. I think we did, too, and the reason that we lost is simply that we were up against a team a bit better than ourselves. The margin of victory was only one goal, but I am not going to try to make any excuses or to suggest that we were unlucky to lose. We had our chances as well as our opponents did, and the fact is that they made better use of theirs than we did of ours.

It is not my place to single out individual players for special praise, and in any case this would hardly be appropriate. Our opponents' great strength was in their teamwork. Their defence was solid, their attack was swift and co-ordinated, and there was a general harmony in the whole side. That is what we were up against, and although I am sorry we lost, I do not think we disgraced ourselves. For my part I thoroughly enjoyed the match.

Finally, I want to say how much we are looking forward to our next meeting. And I must add that although we admit that the better team won this afternoon, we most certainly do not admit that our opponents will necessarily be the better team next time!

But that is in the future. For the present, let us bestow honour where honour is due. I give you the toast of our opponents, the — who, in my opinion, gave one of the finest exhibitions of wing play that we have ever seen on this ground.

### Useful quotations

Do you want people to speak well of you? Then do not speak at all yourself. – *Blaise Pascal*

*See also under* Our Opponents (Cricket).

## Reply to the Toast of our Opponents (Football)

*See under* Our Opponents (Cricket).

### Specimen

Ladies and/or gentlemen – On behalf on my team-mates I thank you most heartily for your generous toast. I fear it was too generous. You have made it appear as if the match was one-sided, yet in fact it seemed to me that you had at least as much of the game as we did. Certainly we had a greater share of the luck, and I should not have been surprised if you had claimed that a draw would have been a fairer result.

But the result is of much less importance than the fact that we all had 90 minutes of hard, good, clean soccer. You have been kind enough to praise us for our teamwork. I am not surprised that you should estimate this most highly, for you made it quite clear by your play that you value it above all individual effort. You made an entirely exaggerated remark about my own performance. Had you been able to see your own play, you would have realised that it will need a much better player than I to surpass the reputation you must have earned among your spectators.

Finally, I must thank you for the very hearty reception and magnificent hospitality that you have given us. Shortly you will be coming to visit us. We shall try to return your hospitality as well as we can. If we can beat you again, we shall do so, but we know that it will be at least as hard a task as it was this afternoon.

On behalf of— Club, I thank you.

# The Teams

Sometimes the toast of both teams together is proposed, and this is especially appropriate when there has been a big margin of victory. The following specimen can be adopted to be used for any team sport.

## *Specimen*

Ladies and gentlemen – It gives me very great pleasure to propose the toast of the two teams who have entertained us so well this afternoon. I think everyone who saw the match will agree that it was a splendid game. Of course one team won and the other lost, but I think the winners will forgive me if I say that although they deserve our congratulations for their very fine performance, the result was not the most important part of the afternoon. What pleased me most – and I think I am speaking for all the spectators – was the fine spirit in which the game was played. It was hard fought, yet always in the highest sporting tradition. The winners never relaxed until the game was over – and the losers gallantly carried the struggle on right up to the end.

It is not my place to single out individual players on either side, and in any case I think this would give a false idea of the match. Both sides played as teams, and the outstanding feature of the game was the high quality of

the teamwork on both sides. Yet two players, I think,
deserve just a word of special mention. I refer, of course,
to the two captains. Each played a capital game, and each
gave his side fine leadership.

Now, I ask you to drink to the health of the two teams,
— and —.

## Success to the Club (Cricket)

This is a common toast at the annual club dinner, and is
generally proposed by the chairman. The speech should
include tributes to the secretary (who will reply to the toast)
and other officials, and also to the captain. Unless there has
been an exceptionally outstanding player, it is not advisable to
single out individual members of the team for special
mention, for obvious reasons. However, any success by a club
member in representative or other such matches should be
mentioned out of courtesy.

### *Specimen*

Ladies and gentlemen – It is my happy duty to rise and
remind you of the success the club has enjoyed during
the season that has just ended, and to ask you to join me
in drinking to continued success in the future.

You do not want me to review our achievements this
season. They have already been placed on record, and we
can feel justly proud of them. Our First Eleven has won 12
matches, and lost only two. Of the six matches that were
drawn, we may fairly say that the weather robbed us of
victory at least three times. But I think we have little
cause for complaint about the weather this season. It has
not been a good summer – English summers rarely are –
but a kind Providence has saved most of the rain for
weekdays and most of the sun for weekends.

I know you will all support me when I pay tribute to
the work of our most energetic secretary and the other
officials who have given so freely of their time to make the
season the success it has been. It would be invidious if I
were to single out any members of the team for special
mention, because our victories have been won more by

teamwork than anything else, and every man has played his part. But I do not think anyone will object when I remind you of the splendid example set by our captain, —, who has excelled not only as a fine all-rounder, but also in the sort of leadership that cricket needs. He has been an inspiration to the team. I must also mention the success of one of our younger players, —, in being chosen to play as an amateur for the county. As you all know, — has now signed professional forms with the county, and next season he will be lost to us. Of course we shall miss him, but we shall take pride in his future career, and we wish him all the success he deserves.

Our Second Eleven has enjoyed less success in actual matches, but its prospects for the future are bright. There has been a welcome influx of youth into the club, and several youngsters have shown in their first season that they will soon be clamouring for places in the First Eleven.

You have already seen the report of the club's financial position, and will have observed that we are still solvent. We never want to be much more, but a little extra cash in hand is necessary if we are to keep up our present standard of equipment. As a result of increased costs we have been obliged to raise the subscription for honorary members from — to —. No one wants to raise the subscription for playing members, and it is because we are anxious to avoid this that I am taking the liberty of reminding you that the nominal honorary subscription is a minimum sum. Any individual additions to it will be most gratefully received.

Cricket is an old English game. It is essentially English and it is by far the oldest of our popular sports. But let us not forget that it was first played – I might almost say invented – by boys. Young lads were wielding home-made bats in the days of Queen Elizabeth I, when their elders look down on the sport as a childish pastime. Now, of course, it is the sport for men and women of all ages. We ourselves should be hard put if we had to manage without our veterans, but let us remember that cricket is also the game for youth. Ours is quite an old club, but it is young in spirit. As I have said, we have some very promising young players; but we need more, and it is up to we older members to do our best to attract youngsters to join us.

Now, ladies and gentlemen, I ask you to join me in drinking to the future success of the club, and with this toast I couple the name of our Honorary Secretary, —.

### Useful quotations

*See under* Our Opponents (Cricket).

# Reply to the Toast of Success to the Club

This speech is made by the honorary secretary, and usually ends with a toast to the captain of the club.

## Specimen

Mr Chairman (or Madam Chair), ladies and gentlemen. Much as I appreciate the honour you have paid me of coupling my name with this toast, I feel unable to accept your compliments on my own behalf alone. On occasions like this the secretary gets all the credit, but in fact this secretary deserves very little of it. The success and smooth running of the club during the season that has just ended were due to the work of the committee, of which I am only one member. Teamwork brought the club its success on the field of play, and teamwork was also responsible for the efficient way in which the club has been run off the field.

I must hasten to assure you that I am not trying to shift the blame for my own shortcomings on to the committee. I do not suggest that it was teamwork that caused the misunderstanding at Easter, when we arrived at our opponents' ground at just the same time as they arrived at ours. That was not the fault of the committee. The blame was all mine – although I can pass a little on to Telecom, because really the telephone line was bad. For the things that went smoothly the Committee deserve your praise; for the tragedies and disasters, blame me.

I should like to add my personal support to your words, Mr Chairman, about our captain. — is not only a fine player and a fine leader, but he is also a fine coach. I have seen him at the nets, putting the youngsters through their paces, and I have seen him giving fielding practice to the team. I have no doubt that the improvement in our standard of match play owes a tremendous amount to the work put in by our captain in coaching and practice.

In thanking you again, therefore, I ask you, ladies and gentlemen, to rise again, and drink to the health of our captain, —. May he have a very long innings.

## Reply to the Toast of the Club Captain (Cricket)

### *Specimen*

Mr Chairman (or Madam Chair), ladies and gentlemen. Thank you for your kindness. It should be easy for me to reply to this toast, because I have only to tell you the truth about the way our team has pulled together and the little that has been required of the captain. Unfortunately, with a rather blatant disregard for the truth, my friend the secretary has anticipated this reply, twisted it to suit his own purpose and modestly sheltered behind it an attempt to prove that his job was equally simple. I am sure you have not been fooled, and I am sure that the other members of our hard-working committee will agree with me when I say that the club owes more to its secretary than to any other member.

I am not so modest as the secretary, and I am going to say quite brazenly that in one respect at least I think I have carried out my duties as captain extraordinarily well. I must make this boast, because quite unaccountably, neither you, Mr Chairman, nor the secretary, has even bothered to mention this most important triumph of mine. As you know, we have played 20 matches during the season, and I, as captain, have won the toss no less than 15 times! This, I submit, is a proud record. It is the best thing I have done for the club. And I would remind you that I did it all off my own bat. It was a personal achievement that owed nothing to teamwork.

But I am afraid it has been my only personal achievement. Teamwork has done all the rest. I can only say it has been a great honour for me to captain such a team, which deserves our most hearty congratulations. Thank you.

# Success to the Club (Football)

*See under* Success to the Club (Cricket).

## *Specimen*

Ladies and gentlemen – I believe it was the late Lord Kinnaird, an early president of the FA, who once celebrated a cup final victory by standing on his head in front of the pavilion at the Oval. As he always played in long white flannels and a cricket cap and had a flowing red beard it must have been a colourful sight. Sometimes it is said that soccer has lost some of its colour, but that is said of most things. We are constantly being told that we live in a drab world, as if the world was never drab in the past. But can anyone fairly say that soccer today is drab? Whatever it was once, is it not now the most exciting and exhilarating game that was ever invented?

Of course, it was not invented really. It just happened and, like Topsy, just growed. Like nearly every other sport, it was started in England. Now it is played all over the world. British players took it abroad and taught other countries to play. Now, it happens that sometimes the pupils beat the masters, and a great groan goes up about the decline of British soccer. Once upon a time British teams could go across the Channel and rattle up cricket scores against teams that had little idea of the game. Is there any need to regret the passing of those days? I don't think so. Nor do I think that British soccer has declined. It is simply that other countries have improved, and the main reason for their improvement has been that British coaches went and taught them the game. Of course we want to win, but even if we do get beaten sometimes, let us rejoice that we have opponents who can now give us a good, hard game.

But my toast is not to the success of soccer in general, or even of British soccer; it is to the success of the club. It is a toast that I can propose with great confidence after the success we have enjoyed during the season that has just ended. You all know our record, and I am sure that you will all join with me in congratulating the team very heartily on its splendid performance. When I say the team I mean the whole team, and I am not going to mention individuals. At least, I am only going to name one, and I name him not so much for his playing – magnificent as it was – as for his leadership. Our captain, —, has inspired the team to play as a team. He has set an example by his own unselfish play, and it is to a great extent due to him that 11 individuals have played the game like one man.

I must say a word also about —, the captain of our Second Eleven. It has been his task to encourage and help the younger members of the club, and the results of his work are already beginning to show. Several of the youngsters are now knocking loudly at the First Eleven door, and the fine form shown by the Second Eleven is the surest sign that the future of the club is going to be at least as good as the past.

Finally, I want to remind you of the great work done by the club officials, and especially the secretary. It was all behind the scenes, but it was worth many goals to us. And that is why, when I ask you to drink this toast, I couple with it the name of —. Ladies and gentlemen, success to the club!

## *Useful quotations*
*See under* Our Opponents (Cricket).

# Success to the Club (Lawn Tennis)

*See under* Success to the Club (Cricket).

## *Specimen*
Ladies and gentlemen – In proposing the toast of success to the club, I think I can do no better than express the hope that the club will enjoy as much success next season

as it did during the season that has just ended. In only one respect can I hope for something better – and that, of course, is the weather. But I am not going to stress this point too much, because although the weather could be better than it was this year, I need hardly remind you that it has sometimes been a good deal worse.

I think I am voicing the general opinion when I say that we have all had a most enjoyable season. On the courts there was never a dull moment. (Insert here any amusing incident that occurred during the season.)

We have put up a good show in club matches, and our own tournaments have been more successful than ever. I am sure you will all join me in congratulating our new champions (insert the names of singles and doubles champions).

We are sorry that we are losing two of our oldest members, who are moving to another district. Both — and — have served the club well, and we wish them every success in the game in the future. A happier matter is the admission of several youngsters who, I hope, will shortly be putting their parents in their place.

Finally, I want to pay my tribute to the club officials, and especially our energetic secretary , who have worked hard so that we could play.

Ladies and gentlemen, I give you the toast – success to the club!

## Useful quotations

Personally, I have always looked on cricket as organised loafing. – *William Temple*

They also serve who only stand and wait. – *John Milton*

*See also under* Our Opponents (Cricket).

# The Gold Medallist (Golf)

Golf is, of course, one of the most individualist sports, and this speech should be frankly in praise of the winner of the prize. Humour is essential, and the speaker should try to include an original golf.

## *Specimen*

Ladies and gentlemen – I am very happy to propose the health of the winner of the Gold Medal, because only a week ago he was my companion in adversity. Actually he was my opponent, but we happened to share the same bunker. I am not going to pretend that our comradeship lasted for long. — deserted me with quite unseemly haste and I was left to continue the excavations by myself. But after the game – and I shan't tell you the result – he expressed his entire agreement with me that the bunker in question – you are all familiar with it, I am sure – ought to be removed.

It is a peculiar thing, ladies and gentlemen, that I do not think there is anyone here with whom I have played who has not voiced the same opinion. I won't say you have all kept to that opinion, I will even admit that on occasions – rare ones, I'm afraid – I myself have regarded that bunker with a most benevolent eye, but by and large there is a general unanimity of opinion that whoever put that bunker there had a grudge against us. Yet the bunker remains, and I have not yet heard anyone make a formal proposal that it should be removed.

I suppose that every club has its pet hazard of this kind, and for all it has cost us I think you will agree that the course would not be the same without it. I am reminded of a cartoon that appeared in *Punch* many years ago, when the late Benito Mussolini was unchallenged dictator of Italy. The cartoon was inspired by the news that Mussolini was spending a holiday playing golf. It depicted him with his ball lying badly, and a monstrous bunker in front. Mussolini was standing in his most dictatorial pose, saying sternly to his caddie, 'Remove that bunker!'

The moral, I suppose, is that golf is no game for dictators. It makes you modest. But I do not think — needed to take up golf to acquire modesty. He was born modest, and his behaviour after carrying off the Gold Medal has been almost apologetic. He has even been heard to say that it was a fluke. All of you who have seen him play, and those of you who have had the chastening experience of playing against him, will, I know, deny that suggestion indignantly. He was a worthy winner, and he thoroughly deserved his success. Ladies and gentlemen – the winner of the Gold Medal!

### *Useful quotations*

Gentlemen with broad chests and ambitious intentions do sometimes disappoint their friends by failing to carry the world before them. – *T.S. Eliot*

There be some sports are painful, and their labour Delight in them sets off. – *William Shakespeare*

*See also under* Our Opponents (Cricket).

## Reply to the Toast of the Gold Medallist (Golf)

### *Specimen*

Ladies and gentlemen – I feel greatly honoured by your kind reception of this toast. I do not deserve it, any more than I deserve the prize that I happen to have won. There are many golfers here who play a much better game than I do.

If possible, I am even worse at speaking than I am at golf. I have had my attacks of nerves when addressing a ball, but they were nothing compared with my feelings on addressing you now. So I am going to try to hole out in one, and just tell you a little story and then sit down. (Insert a suitable story.)

And with that, ladies and gentlemen, I ask you to excuse me. Again, many thanks for your kind toast.

### *Useful quotations*
*See under* Our Opponents (Cricket).

## Success to the Rowing Club

Most of the hints given already in this chapter will prove useful for this toast.

### *Specimen*

Ladies and gentlemen – Before I ask you to drink to the success of the club, I must beg you to approve an expression of thanks to two people. One is our secretary, who not only organised everything with great success throughout the season, but who also arranged this excellent dinner. The other person to whom we are indebted is the clerk of the weather, who gave us some bad breaks at times, but smiled on us in the end.

I'm not going to repeat the results of the events in which we have competed, because you know them already. We have by no means disgraced ourselves, and I am sure that our standard will be at least as high next year.

The object of rowing is, of course, to win the race. But it is the race rather than the victory that counts most, and collecting trophies has its limitations as a pastime. We believe that rowing is a grand sport. I am not trying to under-rate the importance of the competitive element, but I do think you will agree when I say that it is the competition itself rather than the result that gives the greatest pleasure.

So, ladies and gentlemen, when I ask you to drink to our future success, I should like to think of that word 'success' in its broadest sense. Now, ladies and gentlemen, raise your glasses, please, and let us drink the toast – success to the club!

## Report of the Club Secretary

This is a business speech which may be adapted for any sports club. There is no call for oratory or eloquence. The speech should be factual, and should not include long humorous anecdotes, although a little humour is permissible.

## Specimen

Mr Chairman (or Madam Chair), ladies and gentlemen. My report for the season that has just ended will not take long to read. There is no need for me to repeat our match record, for this has already been put up in the clubroom. I know that you will agree that it is a good one.

Our membership now stands at —; — members have resigned after leaving the district or for other reasons, and — new members have been elected. Our future policy with regard to new members will be discussed later.

Finance continues to be our biggest headache. You will have seen the statement of accounts prepared by our treasurer, and if you compare this with last season's statement you will see that we have had to pay more for many items and yet have not had any corresponding increase in revenue. I do not want to be alarmist, but I must point out that we shall have to face up to a choice between raising subscriptions or making some economies. That also is a matter that is down for later discussion.

The extension to the pavilion, which was completed at the beginning of the season, has largely solved our previous problem of accommodation for visiting teams, and I do not think any further improvements in this direction will be needed for a time.

We have arranged a few social events for the winter, and the dates of these will be notified to members within the next few days.

Finally, I should like to remind you of the considerable amount of volunteer work done during the season. Many members have given up their time to serve teas, and there was a big response to my appeal for help on the ground.

In preparation for next season I am going to ask the meeting to authorise me to spend £— on the following new equipment (give details). Whether we can afford that sum is for the meeting to decide, but I must explain that it is necessary if we are to have the same standard of equipment next season as we have had this year.

That is my report, ladies and gentlemen.

# CHAPTER TWELVE

# Business Speeches

## Chairperson's Speech at an Annual General Meeting

This speech will include a brief review of the year's trading, and the chair is required only to give the facts. Attempt at oratory would be out of place, but the chairperson might wish to offer an opinion on the future of the company.

### *Specimen*

Ladies and gentlemen – Before we proceed to the business of this meeting, I have two matters of personal interest to mention. The first is a sad one. I must remind you of the loss we have sustained through the death of —. As you know — was one of our oldest directors, and he served us well in good times and bad. We shall feel the loss of his wise counsel and shrewd foresight; and still more we shall miss a loyal and sincere friend. On this occasion I should like to record our deep sympathy for his family. (Pause.)

The other personal matter to which I must draw your attention is of a happier kind. It is that —, who has been a director for — years, has been elected a Member of Parliament. I am sure that you will want me, on behalf of the meeting, to congratulate — most warmly. Happily the nation's gain will not be our loss; for although — will have less time to spend on the company's affairs, he is remaining on the board and will continue to give us the benefit of his considerable experience and ability.

Last year's trading, as you will see, was satisfactory from every point of view. Our net profits amounted to £—, which represents an increase of £— on the previous year. Provision for taxation required £— as compared with £— for the previous year. With the amount brought forward there is available for distribution the sum of £—.

A final dividend of 50 per cent, making 65 per cent (less tax) on ordinary share capital is proposed. This will absorb £—. After appropriations the carry forward is £—. Our total reserves, including capital reserves, now amount to £—. This represents an increase of £—.

(Now follow with a review of the past year's history relating to buildings, plant, new projects, exports, etc.)

You will see that the volume of our business has risen by over 20 per cent. It is difficult to forecast business conditions in the coming year, but provided that the supply of raw materials is undisturbed, and that prices remain at their present level, there is every reason to believe that our profits will be at least maintained and possibly increased.

During the last year much modernisation has been carried out, and in spite of the considerable outlay it is our belief that this has already proved an excellent investment. Further modernisation still waits to be done, and it is our intention to continue this policy as circumstances permit.

Our employees now number —. Apart from the normal replacements, there have been comparatively few changes of staff during the year. We give a lot of thought to the well-being of our staff, and our Welfare Department has provided (give details). There is a healthy team spirit among the employees of the company, and I am sure you will wish to join with me in expressing our appreciation of the devotion and loyalty of our staff.

# Proposal for the Election of a Director of a Company

This speech is usually made by the chairperson.

## *Specimen*

Ladies and gentlemen – I have the agreeable task of proposing that a directorship be awarded to —. As you know, — has served the company for — years, and during the last — years he has held the position of Works Manager. To say that he has carried out his duties efficiently would be an understatement. Not only has he given the company the benefit of his considerable ability, but he has also displayed a rare devotion and personal enthusiasm for his work. — has shown considerable initiative as well as executive powers, and I am convinced that it is in the best interests of the company that he should now be rewarded with a directorship.

# Trade Union Secretary's Report on the Year's Work

A secretary's job is to state the facts clearly and concisely, and no special eloquence is required for this speech. The subject matter will, of course, depend upon the circumstances and the following specimen might have to be considerably adapted.

## *Specimen*

Mr Chairman (or Madam Chair), ladies and gentlemen. The activities of the union on behalf of its members during the last year are well known to you, and I do not need to go over them again here. I have, however, a few matters to report. One is that our membership has increased by —, bringing the total up to —. This, of course, is the highest number we have ever had in the union. In the course of the year we held — meetings, at which the attendances were slightly higher than in the previous year. Our social activities have been increased, and as a result of their popularity it is intended that they should be further expanded next year.

You will have seen the general state of our finances

from the copies of the balance sheet that have been circulated. There are one or two items, however, on which you would probably like a few words of explanation. (Here explain expenditure as appropriate.)

I do not need to make any comment on the matter of (insert some local topic), which was the most important of our activities during the year. As you know, the union's just claims in this matter were completely met in the end, and our thanks are due to — and —, who carried out the negotiations for us with great energy and perseverance. The matter of (insert some relevant topic) is still pending, as you know. I expect that this will be discussed later during the meeting.

## Speech at a Trade Union Meeting

The specimen below is a fairly typical speech that can be adapted for many different sets of circumstances. The speaker should not try to be over-eloquent, but should simply state his or her points clearly, briefly and bluntly.

### *Specimen*

Mr Chairman (or Madam Chair) and comrades – There seems to be general agreement among us that we should take vigorous action in the matter of (insert some relevant topic), which was sprung on us unexpectedly by —. The only question on which we are not agreed is what form this action should take.

My first point is that our action must be swift and vigorous, or else there will be danger of an unofficial strike. Please do not misunderstand me when I call this a danger. I am not using the word in the sense that it is often used in certain sections of the press. I mean that an unofficial strike would be a danger to us. It would undermine the power of the union, and that must be avoided at all costs.

My second point is that our action, although swift, should not be hasty. Now I know that — has forced this crisis by a hasty and ill-considered action, and that there has been serious provocation. I am not suggesting that we should take it lying down. We have got to stand up for our rights – but let us show more wisdom than they have done. Already the public is generally sympathetic towards us on this matter, in spite of misrepresentation of the issue. If we can keep and increase this public sympathy, we shall win the dispute almost without a fight. The way to do this, I think, is to make a clear and definite statement of our case, and to ensure that it gets the widest publicity. Let us make it plain that we entirely reject —'s statement; but in the first instance, at least, let us put our side of the matter in a sensible and reasoned way. If we do this I think we shall win the case, uphold the authority of the union and retain public sympathy all at the same time. If we can achieve this, it will be a sure guarantee against any future crisis of this sort.

I therefore propose that we should now (follow with the details of the proposal, stating points to be made and procedure to be followed).

## The Prosperity of the Firm

This toast, usually proposed at the annual staff dinner or similar function, comes from an employee. A good deal of care must be taken if the speech is to sound both appreciative and sincere. Fulsome flattery of the heads of the firm would be entirely out of place, and would merely cause embarrassment all round. Similarly there should be no suggestion of servility or obsequiousness in the speaker's remarks. But the speech should reflect appreciation and respect in a healthy form.

### *Specimen*

Mr Chairman (or Madam Chair), ladies and gentlemen. I can say in all sincerity that I am very pleased to have the honour or proposing the toast of the firm. This is not merely because I have dined well – although I certainly have – or even because I have wined well – and again, this is no less than the truth. But the thing that makes it so easy and, indeed, pleasurable a task is simply that it is out of office hours. The firm is, at the moment, a sort of illusion. Seeing all my colleagues here, without their folders and notebooks, computers and telephones, makes me forget the sordid realities of commercial life. Only for the moment, of course. Now if you had asked me to propose the health of the firm at 5.30 this afternoon, or if you were to ask me to do it at 9.30 in the morning, I should say – well, never mind what I would say. In any case that's no reflection on the firm. It's just the matter of the condition of my liver.

Now I have been with the firm for 20 years. I expect to be here another 20. (I thank you for your reception of that threat.) That will make 40 years altogether. Now I ask you, why should I spend nearly the whole of my working life in the service of one firm? There are only two possible answers. The obvious one, of course, is that I couldn't get another job. The alternative, which I greatly prefer, is that I don't want another job. I like it here.

I'm not going to pretend that I'm one of those rare birds who live for their work. I work for my living. But as working hours make up quite a large proportion of living hours, it seems important that one should be satisfied in one's job. And that satisfaction, very largely, depends on one's firm. I think this is a good firm. I like the atmosphere, I like my colleagues, and I like my bosses. I feel that I have a stake in the firm. So ladies and gentlemen, I ask you to join me in drinking to its continued prosperity. The Firm!

## Useful quotations

Work, according to my feeling, is as necessary as eating and sleeping. – *Humboldt*

Many men have been capable of doing a wise thing, many more a cunning thing, but very few a generous thing. – *Alexander Pope*

Corporations have no souls. – *Edward Thurlow*

Work is the grand cure for all the maladies and miseries that ever beset mankind – honest work. – *Thomas Carlyle*

Man's record upon this wild world is the record of work, and of work alone. – *Holland*

No man has a right to be idle if he can get work to do,

even if he be as rich as Croesus. – *Holland*

We have a certain work to do for our bread, and that is to be done strenuously; other work for our delight, and that is to be done heartily; neither is to be done by halves or shifts. – *John Ruskin*

In all the world there is nothing so remarkable as a great man, nothing so rare, nothing so well repays study. – *Parker*

# Reply to the Toast of the Prosperity of the Firm

This speech should be made by the senior director present. It should include a refutation of any generous remarks of a personal nature that may have been made by the previous speaker, and an appreciation of the work done by the staff. The importance of team work is the keynote. The speaker must take great care to avoid any suggestion of patronage or condescension on the one hand, and yet should not try to force an atmosphere of over-familiarity on the other.

## *Specimen*

Ladies and gentlemen – I am very happy to reply to the toast of the prosperity of the firm, which has been so generously proposed and so cordially received. This fact alone is, I think, the surest guarantee of our future prosperity. For the success of every organisation, commercial or otherwise, depends primarily on the co-operation of those who run it, and there is no substitute for good relations and teamwork.

So when I thank you for the toast I must thank you also for all that you have done for the firm in the last 12 months. I hope you will always think of the firm not as 'it' but as 'us', because it is a simple fact that every one of us here tonight has a real stake in it.

I am not going to talk shop on an occasion like this, but I do want to remind you once again of a matter of internal policy which is very dear to our hearts. Each member of the firm has his or her own job to do, and although overlapping is encouraged as far as possible, our business is too complicated to allow us to play musical chairs. But we do want your interest, not only in your own particular job, but in the work of the firm as a whole. More than anything else we want your ideas and suggestions for raising our general efficiency even above its present level. I believe that there is nothing that encourages interest and enthusiasm as a feeling that the ideas of the most junior members of the staff are not only always welcomed, but also will always be treated with consideration and respect.

That brings me back to teamwork. I think a good firm should be like a good cricket team, all working together for the common good and yet not aiming an at equality of performance that can only bring about a standard of mediocrity. We are all still individuals with our own particular abilities, and I think that individuality should always be encouraged within the framework of the team.

Finally I have pleasure in announcing (insert good news, such as positive changes to a company bonus scheme.

On behalf of the firm, ladies and gentlemen, I thank you.

### Useful quotations

*See under* The Prosperity of the Firm.

## The Staff

This toast is proposed by one of the directors. It should include an expression of thanks for the work done by the staff, and emphasis on the importance of teamwork. Broadly speaking, it should follow the same lines as the Reply to the Toast of the Prosperity of the Firm. Again, avoid any hint of patronage or condescension, while at the same time being sure not to go to the other extreme of over-familiarity. The toast can be coupled with the name of a long-serving employee, who can then make the reply on behalf of the staff.

## Specimen

Ladies and gentlemen – It is my privilege and pleasure to propose the health of the staff. The reason why it is a pleasure is that I welcome the opportunity to say a few things that I think every day. Whether work is a positive source of enjoyment or merely a necessary evil is a matter of opinion. Personally I think it is a mixture of both. But there can be no doubt that it is a good deal more pleasant – or, if you like, a good deal less unpleasant – if it is done in a spirit of mutual co-operation. We have that spirit here in a very high degree. I hope we shall always keep it.

Now I am not going to make a high-sounding speech about working for the honour and glory of the firm. This is a business house, and we are in business to make money, and you work in the firm with the same primary objective. But, as you have shown, there is no reason why even the sordid job of making money should not be made pleasant, and the way to make it pleasant is to work as a team. Teamwork means loyalty, and I know that no staff could be more loyal. I want you to know that your loyalty is appreciated.

I have talked enough, ladies and gentlemen. I propose the health of the staff, and I couple with this toast the name of our old friend – old in service, but young in spirit, —.

### Useful quotations

In general those who have nothing to say contrive to spend the longest time in doing it. – *J.R. Lovell*

*See also under* The Prosperity of the Firm.

## Reply to the Toast of the Staff

*See under* The Prosperity of the Firm.

### Specimen

Ladies and gentlemen – On behalf of the staff I am happy to reply to this kind toast. It is easy for me to be sincere in my reply, for I have worked here happily for many years. I think my colleagues, old and young, share my happiness, and the fact that we are all so difficult to get rid of explains more than words what we feel about the firm.

I do not want to get sentimental, because it would be untrue if I were to pretend that the firm takes up the whole, or even the major part, of our lives. Like many others here tonight, I am a family man, and my greatest joy is in my home. But there is here, too, something of a family spirit. It is a different sort of family, of course, as it must be, but it exists, and the place would be the poorer without it.

Like everyone else here tonight, I come to work in order to earn my living. But it has always been my simple philosophy that the mere fact that you do something because you have to is no reason for not liking to do it. Ladies and gentlemen, I confess to you that I like my work; or rather it is not so much my work that I like as the atmosphere in which I do it. I think that everyone contributes to that atmosphere; but it would be most ungenerous of me if I did not say that it could not exist without the active encouragement and participation of the directors. If they have a loyal and co-operative staff, it is what they deserve.

On behalf of the staff I thank you.

## Useful quotations
*See under* The Prosperity of the Firm.

# Presentation Speech
# when an Employee Retires

In the specimen it is assumed that the employee is retiring on reaching the age limit. With a very little alteration the speech can be made to serve where an employee is leaving for health reasons or to take another post. The speech must, of course, be complimentary but no so overgenerous that the remarks lose their value.

## Specimen
Ladies and gentlemen – On an occasion such as this our feelings are bound to be mixed. — is leaving us today,

after 30 years' continuous service with the firm, to enjoy a well-deserved retirement. He takes with him our earnest wishes for his continued health and happiness for many years to come. No one would begrudge him the rest he has earned after his years of hard and selfless work. Yet we cannot pretend that we are happy to see him leave us. No one is indispensable, but there are some people it is very difficult to do without, as I fear we are shortly going to discover. We are going to miss our production manager – but much more we are going to miss — the person.

As is natural in an organisation of this kind, our respective relations with — have been varied. To some he has been one of the bosses, to be addressed as Sir. Others have known him just as Mr Smith; and to a few close colleagues he has been plain Jack. But his attitude to us has never reflected these differences. He has treated us all with the same unfailing courtesy and good humour. By his cheerfulness and natural friendliness — has earned the respect of every one of us, and it is with a sense of real loss that we see him go. On behalf of the staff, I have the great pleasure of presenting — with this small token of our esteem and affection. This is a goodbye present, but I hope he will come to see us at times as a friend – if only to look and gloat. —!

### Useful quotations

As a vessel is known by the sound, whether it be cracked or not; so men are proved, by their speeches, whether they be wise or foolish. – *Demosthenes*

*See also under* The Prosperity of the Firm.

## Reply to a Farewell Presentation

The presentation speech will in some measure govern the reply, but it should be simple, quiet and, above all, sincere.

### *Specimen*

Ladies and gentlemen – There is an eastern proverb that says, 'In the hum of the market there is money, but under the cherry tree there is rest.' Well, I have been in the hum of the market for a good long time. There is a cherry tree in my garden, and it is to my garden that I intend to retire – I did not say rest!

It is difficult for me to realise that today I am leaving this firm where I have worked for so many years. I shall, I think, be quite happy without my work, and in spite of —'s kind words I have not the slightest doubt that the work will get along very well without me. I was going to say that I have been only a cog in the machine, but I think a happier and more accurate description would be a member of a team. The small part I have played in this team has been made easy for me by the loyal co-operation I have always received from every other member.

Now my innings has come to an end, but I shall watch the future achievements of the team from a seat in the pavilion. You have given me a splendid souvenir, and I shall always prize this gift and what it stands for. Thank you for your kind present and especially for the kind wishes that have come with it – and good luck to you all!

### Useful quotations

Lost, yesterday, somewhere between sunrise and sunset, two golden hours, each set with sixty diamond minutes. No reward offered for they are gone for ever. – *Horace Mann*

*See also under* The Prosperity of the Firm.

# Presentation Speech to an Employee Getting Married

A great deal depends on how long the employee has been with the firm. It is assumed in the specimen that the employee in question is a man intending to remain on the staff. If, however, he or she is leaving the firm the specimen should be adapted in conjunction with the Presentation Speech on the Occasion of a Retiring Employee.

### Specimen

Ladies and gentlemen – I have two pleasant tasks to perform. One is to offer — our congratulations on the occasion of his marriage. The other is to present him with a small gift from the staff. There is no need for me to say which is the more important of the two jobs. Tomorrow — will go off to be married, and when he returns from his honeymoon we shall see a different man. He will deny it, of course, but he won't deceive any of us.

I have not had the pleasure of meeting the bride, and I can well understand that this pleasure may be long deferred. Not, of course, that — has anything to fear from me, but no doubt he has made out to his wife-to-be that his colleagues are just the sort of people she would wish him to mix with, and he doesn't want to disappoint her. But I am sure that he has made a splendid choice. He always had good taste, and I know that his bride could not have done better. In such circumstances happiness is a foregone conclusion, and I need only to offer our very best wishes to Mr and the future Mrs —.

### Useful quotations

Intemperance in talk makes a dreadful havoc in the heart. – *Wilson*

*See also under* The Bride and Bridegroom.

## Reply to a Presentation Speech on Getting Married

This speech should be brief and light-hearted.

### Specimen

Ladies and gentlemen – On behalf of myself and my fiancée, thank you very much for your kind gift and good wishes. Not all of you have met —, but I hope it won't be too long before you do. Getting married is a big step, but I am sure that I am doing the right thing. I know there are plenty of old hands here who will be able to give me advice and help if I do have any difficulties – indeed, one or two of you have already offered some wise words – but I hope that won't be necessary. You all look well on it, so it can't be that hard! I don't think you will see a different person when I come back from my honeymoon, except that perhaps I shall be happier and more contented. Thanks again for all your kindness.

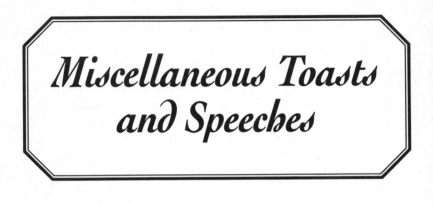

# CHAPTER THIRTEEN

# *Miscellaneous Toasts and Speeches*

## The Press

Very often the speaker begins by making a few mildly critical remarks about the press, just for fun, and then retracts them as the speech continues. This sort of treatment is suitable for an able and experienced speaker, but the novice is advised to play safe and leave out the criticism.

### *Specimen*

Ladies and gentlemen – From time to time one picks up a newspaper and reads a letter from an irate reader complaining about some item, and solemnly informing the editor that although he has been a regular reader for the last 40 years he will never buy the paper again. I often wonder if these correspondents carry out their threats, or if they get over their annoyance. On several occasions I have had the same feelings, not with one paper, but with almost every paper I have read. But one reason why I have got over my annoyance in the end is simply the fact that newspapers print such letters. Indeed the correspondent has only to end up by saying, 'Of course you won't dare to print this' to make absolutely sure of seeing his name in print a few days later.

This, I think, is typical of one of the outstanding

virtues of our newspapers. They are fearless. Of course they give the public what it wants, because a newspaper must sell, but they do not shirk from giving unpalatable news and making unpopular comments when these are thought necessary.

Most of our newspapers are to some extent partisan, and it is a fact that if you read the leading articles of two opposing papers on the same day you might get a very different impression of the way the government is doing its job. But broadly speaking, our newspapers keep the opinions to the leaders, and do not mix them up with the simple reporting of the news. The reader can of course ignore the leaders. But it is most important that they should appear, and the fact that they differ from one another to such an extent is an excellent sign of the health of the press as a whole. In some countries you will find that all the newspapers express the same opinions. This make things much simpler for the readers, of course, but it means that the press is not free. It is in the nature of things for different people to hold different views, and the free expression of conflicting views is precisely what we mean by liberty and democracy. When I read two or three conflicting leaders I am sometimes puzzled, but if I ever find that all the leaders are saying the same thing I shall be seriously alarmed.

It is sometimes said that the press moulds public opinion. Now I do not think that the representatives of the press who are with us tonight will take it amiss if I express the view that it would be nearer the truth to say that public opinion moulds the press. If a citizen has a grievance, if he sees injustice in any department of our social life, his first thought is usually to write to the press. You all know how many important issues have first come to light as a result of letters of this kind. You all know how many times the responsible authority has had to redress an injustice as a result of the publicity given to it in the press. But what none of us knows is how many injustices and abuses in office do not occur because of the existence of a watchful and fearless press. I suspect they are numerous, and for this reason above all the freedom of our press must be held sacred. For the freedom of the press is the guarantee of our own freedom.

Ladies and gentlemen, I ask you to drink to the press and the health of its representatives who are with us tonight, and I couple with this toast the name of —.

## Useful quotations

Four hostile newspapers are to be feared more than a thousand bayonets. – *Napoleon Bonaparte*

With just enough learning to misquote. – *Lord Byron*

Amicably if they can, violently if they must. – *De Quincey*

It is easier to be critical than correct. – *Benjamin Disraeli*

Newspapers are the schoolmasters of the common people. – *Beecher*

The true use of speech is not so much to express our wants as to conceal them. – *Oliver Goldsmith*

In these times we fight for ideas, and newspapers are our fortresses. – *Heinrich Heine*

Newspapers always excite curiosity. No one ever lays one down without a feeling of disappointment. – *Charles Lamb*

# Reply to the Toast of the Press

## Specimen

Ladies and gentlemen – A guilty conscience is a poor thing to have, especially when you are preparing a speech. I had a guilty conscience before I came here tonight. I was told that the health of the press would be proposed. That meant a speech, and knowing the press as I do, and knowing what its own representatives say to one another about it when they get together – knowing all this, I took it for granted that the speech would be at least partly critical. I was asked to reply, and I prepared a reply in advance. In it I answered, as well as I could, the sort of criticism that I expected to be made.

Now my speech is useless, because instead of criticism you have offered only praise. Putting aside my personal discomfiture for the moment, I must say on behalf of the press that I greatly appreciate the things you have said. Of course our press is not perfect by any means, and it will never to anything but imperfect. But I ask you to believe me when I say that most of our faults are not malicious. We try to give the news accurately and without distortion, and when we fail it is usually because of lack of time, poor communications, shortage of space, or some other similar cause. As you know, getting out a newspaper is a hasty business, and haste is the enemy of accuracy. A philosopher might ask, very wisely, 'Why all the rush?' There is no reason, except that you, the public, demand it. If any newspaper decided to defer publication of news for even a few hours, to allow for consideration and double-checking of details, it would soon lose its customers.

I was pleased that the proposer of this toast made the point that public opinion has more influence on the press than the press has on public opinion. It is a common criticism of newspapers that for privately owned concerns they have too much power to make people think along certain lines. This criticism does not flatter the public, and I think it is entirely false. The function of the press is to allow for the free expression of public opinion, not to try to dictate it. The very fact that newspapers are competitive makes them sensitive to public opinion, because it is on the public's opinion of a newspaper that its circulation depends.

This does not mean that we are unconscious of our responsibilities. We know that the press has power. We think it is good that it should have power, so long as it is used to express the views and wishes of the community as a whole, and we shall continue to try to do our duty to the community to the best of our ability.

Ladies and gentlemen, on behalf of the press, I thank you.

# Vote of Thanks to a Lecturer

It is difficult to give general advice on this speech, because its contents and style will depend very largely on the subject of the lecture that has been. For example, a vote of thanks to a professor of archaeology who has lectured on Roman Britain would be entirely different from a vote of thanks to a professional cricketer who has given a talk on spin bowling. The following specimen, which is a vote of thanks to a temperance lecturer, must therefore be regarded as typical only to a limited extent.

## *Specimen*

L adies and gentlemen – I am sure I am speaking on behalf of the whole audience when I sat that — has given us a remarkably instructive, lucid and interesting talk. In my experience lectures on this subject all too often rely on sentimental and emotional appeals. — has certainly not neglected the human aspect of his theme, and indeed he has drawn a vivid and graphic picture of the social and moral effects of alcoholism. But he has based his case on hard facts, and he has marshalled these in a way that to me, at any rate, makes them completely irrefutable. His arguments were entirely free from bigotry and narrow-minded prejudice, and the evidence he has brought forward is as conclusive as it is startling. I am convinced that no one can leave this hall without having been deeply affected by this lecture. Talks of this kind can do more than anything else to combat the evils of drink. It only remains for me to propose a very hearty vote of thanks to — for his admirable lecture.

## *Useful quotations*

Alcohol – liquid madness sold at 10d the quartern. – *Thomas Carlyle*

If abstinence on the part of a temperate drinker would reclaim any drunkard, a man of ordinary humanity would practise it as far as considerations of enjoyment were concerned. – *Lord Bramwell*

# Vote of Thanks to
# an Amateur Dramatic Society

This speech is usually made after a performance by the society. It should be brief, and the speaker should be careful not to single out individual actors and actresses. The speech should always include a generous tribute to the work of the people behind the scenes.

## *Specimen*

Ladies and gentlemen – On behalf of the audience I should like to thank you all for the wonderful show you have given us. We expected it to be good, for we know how enthusiastic you have been in preparing for it. But I am sure that none of us expected the production to be of this high standard. I only wish that some of the London critics had come here and seen what can be done by amateurs who combine enthusiasm and ability in such a high degree.

I am not going to praise any of the cast singly, because if I did that I should in honesty be bound to praise every one of you. You all played your parts superbly. But I hope you will forgive me if I do single out a few members of your society for special mention. They are not on the stage, and indeed we have not seen them, but we have seen the results of their work behind the scenes, and it would be impossible to praise this too highly.

When I add that I wish the society every success in the future I am merely saying that I hope you will soon have another show ready for our delight. Again on behalf of the audience, thank you very much.

# Our Australian Guests

This speech can be adapted for use in proposing the toast to visitors from elsewhere in the former Commonwealth or other countries with close ties with Britain. In all such cases, however, the speech can stress the cross-country links but should always make a point of emphasising the individuality of the country in question.

## *Specimen*

Ladies and gentlemen – Our two nations have always enjoyed the strongest of links, but now that the political structure of those links has changed, I feel that they have been strengthened – not weakened – by the fact that they rest on sounder foundations. We each recognise our individualities and our strengths, yet we choose to maintain a solidarity based on good will and mutual help. We offer an example to the world of how free, democratic peoples, separated from one another by many thousands of kilometres, can live together in a voluntary and mutually beneficial association.

It is within the memory of some of you how the solidarity of that association has twice been sorely tested during this century, and how on each occasion it has gained from the ordeal. Little good comes out of the evils of war, but those of us who were privileged to serve alongside Australian troops gained a new experience in comradeship that will never be forgotten. I do not need to remind you how that spirit has continued in the happier days of peace.

Now – in the days of easy travel and electronic development – as the world, it seems, becomes more accessible, we are proving that the distance between us need not separate us, and that we can work to foster economic and cultural ties between our peoples.

The British are often accused of paying too much attention to sport. We in this country acknowledge the fault, and I think I am right in saying that the Australians also plead guilty to the charge. If the Test Matches mean as much to them as they do to us, then they are very important events indeed. Their true significance goes far beyond the scoreboard. To both of us sport means not only playing a game, but sportsmanship and fair play. The Australians excel at many sports besides cricket; but what arouses our admiration most is their supreme excellence in the quality of sportsmanship.

Ladies and gentlemen, I give you the toast of our Australian guests.

# Our American Guests

In this speech, stress can be placed on the common language and culture, while differences can be considered to show the individuality of the two countries. As a major world power, America's lead role in preserving world peace can be a focus.

## *Specimen*

Ladies and gentlemen – It is my privilege to propose the toast of our American guests. According to the Home Office, I believe they come under the category of aliens. I have never met people less alien in my life. They belong to the same English-speaking family as ourselves, and I hope they will consider themselves at home as long as they are in Britain. In fact, I do not really need to express this hope, for the Americans – themselves so wonderfully hospitable – are quick to relax and accept the hospitality we can offer to them.

The Americans are proud of their way of life, and rightly so. We, too, are proud of ours. Often we compare the two; sometimes to the advantage of one and sometimes to the advantage of the other. Yet although there are many differences, there are more points of similarity, and on the fundamentals – the ideals of decency and freedom and justice – the two peoples are entirely at one.

As commercial links strengthen, an increasing number of people are able to travel to the United States, and electronic networking brings us ever closer together, we are quickly learning and appreciating more about each other's cultures. This can only bring us closer together.

Some amongst you may have personal experience of the close ties fostered between our two countries in two world wars as we fought under a unified command, and shared both setbacks and victory. For others, this may have only been learned from the history books. All of you, however, will be aware of more recent times when America has established the lead role in standing firm against those aggressors who do not share our wish for world peace. History has shown us that the price of peace has been,

and will continue to be, strength of principle and eternal
vigilance. When the need has arisen, our two countries
have proved that they can work together harmoniously
and with considerable effect. I am convinced that our
friendship with the great United States of America is one
of the strongest bulwarks of peace in the world today.

Ladies and gentlemen, I give you the toast of our guests
from the United States.

## Our French Guests

The speaker should stress the alliance with France and the
close cultural and economic bonds.

### *Specimen*

Ladies and gentlemen – It is with very great pleasure
that I rise to greet our guests from France. A great
French writer once said, 'Everyone has two countries: his
own and France.' I should be tempted to say that the
French are unlucky in having only one, but there is
actually no need to be sorry for them, because that one
country is France.

France is our closest neighbour, and I do not mean
merely geographically. The ties that bind our two
countries are very strong in every field of human life. And
we must acknowledge that the French have done much to
prevent us from being more insular than we already are.
Every year thousands of Britons cross that strip of water
that we rather arrogantly call the English Channel, and
spend a holiday in a country that seems to them to be one
huge holiday resort. They come back with happy
memories, and so our common link is strengthened over
and over again.

Many centuries ago we used to fight the French.
Eventually both of us came to our senses, and for a long
time now our two peoples have proved staunch and
permanent allies in peace as well as in war.

Now, with increasing business and commercial ties and
with the development of the European Union, our ties

become ever-closer. And while we each maintain our own invididuality, our nations have proved that they can work together to mutual benefit and success. It is a good omen that the Entente Cordiale has never been more cordial that it is today.

Ladies and gentlemen – I give you the toast of our guests from France.

# In Aid of Charity

This speech will obviously depend to a great extent on the particular charity involved. The specimen has been made on general lines, so that most of it will be of use for almost any occasion of this kind.

## *Specimen*

Ladies and gentlemen – It should be the case that charity appeals are out of date and unneccessary. We have a welfare state. In theory we are all provided for from the cradle to the grave. The hospitals and indeed the whole health service are financed by compulsory insurance and taxation. Unemployment relief, public assistance and pensions are similarly provided.

But of course there is still a need for charities. I don't think anyone will doubt that the charity I am asking you to support today is a good cause, and it is a fact that it cannot continue without private assistance. The subscriptions that we receive today are less than they were, and our costs have greatly increased. You know that nothing is wasted on administrative expenses – indeed a very large part of the work is done voluntarily. Those who do this work are making their contribution, and a very valuable one it is. I ask you to make yours. However small it is, it will be a great help. I do not think you will ever regret having given it.

# *Quips* and *General Wit*

Writing about art is like dancing about architecture.

The best audience is intelligent, well-educated and well-oiled!

I probably don't deserve this – but then I do have arthritis, and I don't deserve that either.

A bachelor never makes the same mistake once.

Bigamy is having one wife too many. Some find monogamy to be same thing.

He doesn't have much to say – but least he doesn't try to say anything else.

Chastity is curable if detected early enough.

Christmas comes – but once a year is enough!

My son has taken up meditation. I suppose that's a step forward from doing nothing!

Dancing is the perpendicular expression of a horizontal desire.

I don't believe we've met. I'm Mr Right!

I'm glad you don't recognise me. I'd much rather have you like me for myself.

Keep a diary and one day it will keep you.

Diplomacy is the art of saying 'Nice doggie, good boy!' – until you find a gun.

He is so perfectly diplomatic that he lets everybody else have his way!

I must get out of these wet clothes and round a dry Martini.

Man is the only animal that blushes – or needs to.

She was just a passing fiancée!

The last time Britain went into Europe with any semblance of success was 6 June 1944.

Between two evils I always pick the one I've never tried before.

The trouble with facts is that there are too many of them.

Nothing is so fallacious as facts except, perhaps, statistics.

A woman who strives to be like a man lacks ambition.

Equality is a myth – woman are better.

Let me share an important discovery with you. Food is an important part of a balanced diet.

The reason good friends are so few? They get to know all about you – and then still have to like you.

Give me rod, balmy blue skies and a beautiful partner – and you can keep the rod and blue skies.

No one ever went broke underestimating the taste of the British public.

They hope to live in a beautiful flat overlooking the rent.

I won't tell anybody how much insurance cover I have with the Pru. What I will say is when I go, they go.

A jury consists of 12 men and true assembled to decide who has the better lawyer.

I've found a great way to start the day – go straight back to bed.

Love is not the dying sigh of a distant violin. It's the triumphant twang of bedspring.

Marriage is not a word, it's a sentence.

Money isn't everything. I've never found it to be enough.

There 's no problem so big that you can't run away from it.

Progress might have been all right to begin with, but already it's gone too far.

Quite by chance I overheard a real pearl of wisdom. My only regret is that I did it my way.

The ladies do have a problem with retirement. They get twice as much husband on half as much money.

You don't have to work very hard to figure out why Robin Hood stole from the rich. The poor had no money.

An after-dinner speech should be like a lady's dress – long enough to cover the subject but brief enough to be interesting.

Before standing to deliver, any speaker would do well to heed an elegant piece of advice. 'Like a love affair any fool can start one, but to end one takes considerable skill.'

A speaker who doesn't strike oil in five minutes should stop boring.

Like babies, speeches are easy to conceive but a whole lot more difficult to deliver.

An after-dinner speaker eats a meal he doesn't want so that he can tell a lot of stories he finds very difficult to remember to a lot of people who almost certainly have already heard them – thankless job.

I've never heard a spontaneous speech that was worth the paper it was written on.

In general terms it takes me about three weeks to polish up a good impromptu speech.

Behind every successful man there stands an annoyed woman who knows better.

There's no secret about success. Every successful man wants to tell you all about it.

To be successful in life you need only ignorance, plenty of confidence and some luck. Anybody who tells you any different is lying.

Franklin D. Roosevelt, President of the United States, gave a very sound piece of advice: never underestimate a man who overestimates himself.

Do you know – he hasn't a single redeeming vice!

Nouveau is better than no riche at all.

If the French were really so clever they would speak English.

The thoughtless are seldom wordless.

It doesn't matter whether you believe you can do something or not, you are right.

Amateurs built the ark, professionals the *Titanic*.

It is always safer to assume not that the old way is wrong but that there may be a better way.

You don't have to destroy the city before you can build the New Jerusalem.

To blind oneself to change is not to halt it.

It takes genius and courage to originate not initiate.

A man's true worth is the good he does in the world.

Money is the wise man's religion.

In the factory we make cosmetics. In the store we sell hope.

Everything comes to he who hustles while he waits.

To be persuasive, we must be believable.
To be believable, we must be credible.
To be credible, we must be truthful.
I wonder how successful salesmen manage it?

The most important sale of your life is that of selling yourself to yourself.

A good salesman is one who sell goods that won't come back to customers that will.

He who has something to sell
And goes and whispers in a well
Is not so apt to make the dollars
As he who climbs the tree and hollers.

This stone marks the spot
Where a notorious sort
Doth lie.
Whether at best or not
It matters not to you or I.

Here lies the body of Paddy O'Pound,
Who was lost at sea and never found.
He angled many a purling brook
But lacked the angler's skill.
He lied about the fish he took
And here he's lying still.

Milk and water sold I ever
Weight and measure gave I never.

Here lieth in honourable position,
The outside case of Thomas Hind, Clockmaker.

Sometimes the wit and wisdom of life are best found on the tablets which mark our departure from this world. Bear in mind that they are written by friends who have nothing to fear in absolute truth.